THE BIG BOOK
OF FLIP CHARTS

Other books in *The Big Book of Business Games* series include:

The Big Book of Business Games
The Big Book of Team Building Games
The Big Book of Presentation Games
The Big Book of Customer Service Training Games
The Big Book of Sales Games
The Big Book of Stress Management Training Games (forthcoming)

THE BIG BOOK OF FLIP CHARTS

A Comprehensive Guide for Presenters, Trainers, and Team Facilitators

Robert William Lucas

McGraw-Hill

New York Chicago San Francisco Lisbon London Madrid
Mexico City Milan New Delhi San Juan Seoul
Singapore Sydney Tokyo

Library of Congress Cataloging-in-Publication Data

Lucas, Robert W.
   The big book of flip charts : a comprehensive guide for
presenters, trainers, and team facilitators / Robert William Lucas.
     p. cm.
   Includes index.
   ISBN 0-07-134311-3
   1. Business presentations Charts, diagrams, etc. 2. Employees-
-Training of Charts, diagrams, etc. 3. Teams in the workplace
Charts, diagrams, etc. I. Title.
   HF5718.22.L83 1999
   658.4'5—dc21   99–31728
                                    CIP

McGraw-Hill

*A Division of The **McGraw·Hill** Companies*

16 17 18 19 DIG/DIG 13

ISBN-13: 978-0-07-134311-4

ISBN-10: 0-07-134311-3

The sponsoring editor for this book was Richard Narramore, the editing supervisor was Paul R. Sobel, and the production supervisor was Elizabeth J. Strange. This book was set in Novarese by Inkwell Publishing Services. Printed and bound by Book Mart.

McGraw-Hill books are available at special quantity discounts to use as premiums and sales promotions, or for use in corporate training programs. For more information, please write to the Director of Special Sales, McGraw-Hill, Two Penn Plaza, New York, NY 10121-2298. Or contact your local bookstore.

Dedicated to my wife and life partner,

M.J.,

who continues to be a loving inspiration and
support for me as I take on projects such as this book.

CONTENTS

CONTENTS

CONTENTS

PART III
25 FLIP CHART ACTIVITIES FOR BRAINSTORMING, ICEBREAKING, TEAM PROBLEM SOLVING, AND FACILITATING MEETINGS

CONTENTS

PART IV
APPENDIXES

INTRODUCTION

Looking for fun and creative new presentation ideas has long been a hobby of mine, and it eventually became a business. For more than 27 years I have used and watched others use flip charts to present information, and each time I find a new flip chart technique, I'm as wide-eyed as the kid in the candy store. I can't wait to get back and try it on my next audience. In my experience what separates the good flip charts from the bad (and in some cases, the ugly!) is always the ability of the facilitator to use creative techniques to share information, the willingness to go beyond simply writing words on flip chart paper. My goal with this book is to do some of the "creative leg work" for you, and to share many of the great ideas I've picked up through the years for creating professional-looking flip charts, delivering impressive presentations, and facilitating group discussions with flip charts. Even though flip charts are not high-tech pieces of equipment—they've have been around for decades—they are extremely flexible tools and can be surprisingly complex and powerful, if they are used thoughtfully. As such, they require a degree of knowledge, ability, and creativity to be used effectively.

WHAT THIS BOOK WILL DO FOR YOU

If you are like me, you are never satisfied with the status quo. I continually look for better mousetraps, or new ways of performing old tasks. It doesn't matter to me how long something has been done a certain way; I am convinced that there has to be a better way of doing it.

In this book, you will encounter many ideas and concepts that you may have seen elsewhere. However, I am betting that you will also find many new and helpful techniques.

As you go through these pages and practice the skills and techniques described, I am convinced that you will be entertained and enlightened about ways to make your presentations more effective, and more fun. (Flip charts can be a lot of fun!)

In each section of the book, I have included strategies, techniques, examples, and illustrations of how to present information visually. I have addressed a variety of presentation situations and provided detailed suggestions on how flip charts can best be used in each. To help you locate flip chart-related materials I have included an accessories and resources section at the end of this book (see Appendix C). I have also included, in Part III, 25 activities that use flip charts to generate interest, participation, and ideas while actively involving participants.

After reading this book, you should be able to:

- Recognize the untapped potential of the flip chart in a learning environment.

- Identify ways to improve the quality of your own flip charts.

- Prepare flip charts that grab and hold the attention of your audience.

- Create flip charts that present information clearly, concisely, and creatively.

- Add simple but impressive graphics to your flip charts.

- Use flip charts to facilitate training sessions and meetings for maximum participant involvement.

SIX REASONS YOU SHOULD BE USING FLIP CHARTS IN YOUR PRESENTATIONS

1. Flip Charts Are the Perfect Medium for Harnessing the Collective Brain Power of a Group

One of the key elements of androgogy (adult learning) is active involvement of the learners. There are two ways to involve your audience with using flip charts: (1) solicit ideas and capture them on a flip chart yourself, or (2) pass out markers and paper and let the participants do their own problem solving and writing. By involving others, you take yourself out of the role of presenter or expert and move into a new role of facilitator. This is a less intimidating and more professional role since you build on the knowledge of the group and avoid talking down to or controlling others. Adult learners like to have input into what happens to, and with, them.

2. Good-Looking Flip Charts Are the Best Visual Aids a Presenter Could Want

I don't know about you, but when I take the time to create professional-looking flip charts to support a presentation, I somehow feel more fulfilled as a presenter. Maybe it's because I don't consider myself artistic or creative, so when I have a finished product that I think looks good, I feel a sense of accomplishment. The feeling is amplified when someone else comments on the quality of my flip charts.

Also, in creating a series of pages for a presentation, I get to practice some of the techniques outlined in this book, which enhances my skills even more. These, of course, are just side benefits. The main reason for using flip charts is that they help the presenter communicate better. Research done by the Wharton School of Business on the effectiveness of using visual aids when presenting, found that using visuals in a presentation can cut meeting time by 24 percent. Here's what the study found:

- When visuals were used, audience members perceived presenters to be more effective. Typical comments following presentations were *better prepared, more concise, clearer, more interesting.*

- Following a visually supported presentation, 64 percent of participants were able to make a decision quicker. Those in nonvisual supported groups took longer to make a decision.

- Of those audience members in a visual presentation, 79 percent reached consensus, compared to 58 percent in a group with no visual support.

- Of the participants in a visual presentation, 67 percent found the presenter convincing, compared with 50 percent in the group without visual support.

If you have ever tried to take notes as someone rattles on, seemingly oblivious to the audience, you will understand the value of flip charts. Because participants can refer to a posted flip chart page without interrupting to ask the facilitator to repeat a point, they are able to review material or catch up at their own speed. In addition, flip charts provide a vehicle for reinforcing what participants heard, or thought they heard.

Many times following a meeting, you may need to transfer the information you have gathered so that it can be analyzed, condensed, or forwarded to others. For example, as part of a needs assessment I participated in earlier this year, I facilitated numerous focus groups of supervisory personnel for an organization. At the end of the sessions, I had to transfer the information to a computer file, forward copies to various members of management, tally and analyze results, and then help produce a report to upper management along with recommendations. The executive overview included direct quotes captured on the flip charts during the meetings. Without the flip charted comments from the meeting, this would not have been possible.

3. Giving Meeting Participants a Chance to Write on Flip Charts Increases Their Interest and Learning

Years ago, I came across statistics related to how we retain information. One study showed that retention increases over a three-day period when active learning (participant involvement) is used.

Specifically, we remember:

- 10 percent of what we read only
- 20 percent of what is heard only
- 30 percent of what is seen only
- 50 percent of what is seen and heard
- 70 percent of what is said
- 90 percent of what is said and done

Confucius (551–479 B.C.) offers another take on these numbers:

I hear; I forget
I see; I remember
I do; I understand.

The message here is that even though you may get some of your message across through speaking or demonstrating, getting your participants actively involved increases the likelihood that learning will take place.

4. Flip Charts Are Simple and Inexpensive to Use

Flip charts have long been the hands-down favorite of presenters. They are versatile, simple to set up and use, and convenient for capturing ideas quickly; they require no cords or electrical outlets, are relatively inexpensive compared with other visual aids, and can be used virtually anywhere. With flip charts, gone is the worry and expense of having to carry an overhead projector, bulbs, extension cords, screens, and other accessories. You do not even have to supply an easel to use them. With masking tape, straight pins, and/or clips, you can turn nearly any wall surface into a writing surface. As a result, virtually any large room or open space can be converted into an ideal presenter's forum.

5. Flip Charts Facilitate Creativity

I thoroughly enjoy the opportunity to prepare flip charts for a presentation. Even though preparation can be time consuming, it allows you to express your personality and ideas on paper. Unlike computer programs, which limit you to the graphic and text images included in the software (unless you are a computer wizard and can create your own stuff), flip charts free you to become as creative as you like. You are limited only by your imagination (and the time and resources you have available). One of the most creative techniques I've discovered in a while comes from an acquaintance—Linda Wells of Lubbock, Texas. Linda begins by using large cotton balls to coat a flip chart page with food coloring. She then dips a large cotton-tip swab in household bleach to draw letters and images on the colored paper. The result is a "reverse image" that is truly eye-catching and unique.

Throughout this book, I have included sample graphic images, ideas, and suggestions for really "jazzing up" your flip chart pages. By no means do I consider skilled at drawing or visually creative in laying out information and images. However, I have learned over my professional career what works.

To enhance your own flip chart skills, I encourage you to take opportunities to practice whenever possible. Pick a couple of images or characters you like from this book, or another source. Once you have a few ideas, doodle whenever you have time. Draw the images on scraps of paper, restaurant napkins—any writing surface you can find. Pretty soon, you'll be able to replicate the images on your flip chart pages with little effort. Remember, your participants are not art critics (well ... most are not).

6. Flip Charts Provide a Vehicle for Spontaneity

Whenever I see someone jump up to write on a flip chart at a meeting, I suspect that they are a current or former trainer (or maybe an only child like me who enjoys the limelight!).

It is so easy to grab a marker and start writing ideas or capturing participant comments.

This is one of the many reasons that I support the practice of having a flip chart in every meeting and training session. You never know when an opportunity to make an idea visual may occur. As you'll see in other sections of this book, there are literally hundreds of things you can do with a flip chart and a couple of markers.

Whether you are brainstorming by using one of the 25 activities in Part III of this book, or simply facilitating the flow of a discussion by visually presenting key points, you will find flip charts to be one of the most powerful tools available.

TWO KEYS TO FLIP CHART SUCCESS

I have found two techniques to be particularly helpful in presenting a professional image and making presentations with flip charts easier. And these are ideas that most of us were taught as children:

1. *Gather and organize all your toys.* Translated, this means make sure you have the materials and information you will need for the session before participants arrive. I cover the concept of a trainer's tool box and its contents in Chapter 4. For now just think about what you will need to communicate your message effectively and arrange to have it for the session or meeting. Aids include handouts, additional audiovisual equipment, accessories, posters, and anything else that will help participants understand what you are trying to share with them.

2. *If you are going to play with the toys, read the instructions first.* This part is crucial. Presenting information on a flip chart is simple, but it is also an art, and can be done beautifully or poorly. Spend some time to learn the "rules of the game." You'll be surprised at how a small investment of time can pay satisfying dividends during your next presentation.

As you read this book and think about designing your own flip charts, remember this easy test for effectiveness of your visuals:

- Are they clear?
- Are they concise?
- Are they simple?
- Are they graphic?

If you can answer yes to all four questions, you're on you way to creating successful presentations supported by flip charts!

Finally, let me say that I have had more fun writing this book than any of my previous ones. Researching creative techniques, talking to people about their ideas, and trying things out—all have been a real treat, an education, and an opportunity. I hope that reading and using the techniques included proves to be as equally as much fun for you. I would love to hear your comments and suggestions, and any additional ideas you have for using flip charts. Feel free to contact me if you want to provide feedback, ask questions, or just chat.

Bob Lucas
Creative Presentation Resources, Inc.
P.O. Box 180487
Casselberry, FL 32718-0487
E-mail: blucas@PresentationResources.net
Web: www.PresentationResources.net

Happy flip charting!

Bob Lucas

ACKNOWLEDGMENTS

I have heard it said that there are no original ideas, only variations on themes. To that end, I owe all the knowledge outlined in this book to the marvelous trainers and facilitators who have shared their expertise and thoughts on to effective training and presentations with me over the past 26 years. Without their input and ideas, I could not have created this comprehensive resource on flip charting.

It is my hope that all those reading *The Big Book of Flip Charts* will benefit from the ideas included and will in turn pass on their knowledge to future generations of trainers, facilitators, presenters, and managers.

Special thanks go to Richard Narramore, senior editor at McGraw-Hill, for his guidance and patience during the creation of this book.

THE BIG BOOK
OF FLIP CHARTS

Part I

HOW TO DRAW GREAT-LOOKING FLIP CHARTS

Chapter 1

Basic Layout and Design Principles

A simple way to approach flip chart design is to think of a phrase summarizing your topic that will grab the audience's attention. Next, condense the details of that concept down to the fewest words necessary to convey the thought. Finally, decide on a graphic image that will complement the words and enhance the message. Two techniques described later in the book—mind mapping and storyboarding—can help.

Suppose you are trying to convey the fact that a 1997 study on employment litigation by the Society for Human Resource Management (SHRM) found the following:

1. Of 4900 human resource professionals surveyed, 6 of 10 reported lawsuits in their organization within the past five years.
2. Fifty-seven percent said that their organization has been sued at least once during that period.
3. Twenty-three percent reported lawsuits in recent years.
4. Of the lawsuits reported, 11 percent involved sexual discrimination or equal pay disputes, and 14 percent involved sexual harassment.

To flip-chart this information, select a title line, then decide how to succinctly lay the information out visually to aid understanding. Your chart might look like this:

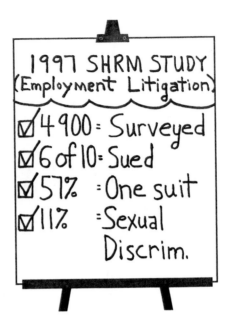

You have now used symbols and abbreviations to significantly reduce the number of words needed. Also, you have created a visual that is easy to follow.

The key is to distribute your text and images equally so that a balance is maintained. One rule of thumb for combining images and text is to create a C shape (it could also be a backward C with the various blocks of text and images on your flip chart, as shown below:

ARRANGE TEXT AND GRAPHICS IN LETTER PATTERNS

The visual pattern of words and text you create is referred to as an *arrangement*. Simplicity is the key when arranging your flip chart ideas. Do not clutter your page with too much information, color, or imagery. Leave plenty of white space so that your participants' attention is not pulled in conflicting directions. When laying out material on your page, select a pattern that resembles one of the following letters:

C, O, S, Z, L, or T

Typically, material displayed in the informal C, S, Z, or T pattern shown in the examples appears more dynamic, and will likely catch your participants' eye. Whatever pattern you choose, remember that the focus should be the message (words), not the graphics. Images that are too large overpower the message and defeat their purpose. They should be reduced or simplified.

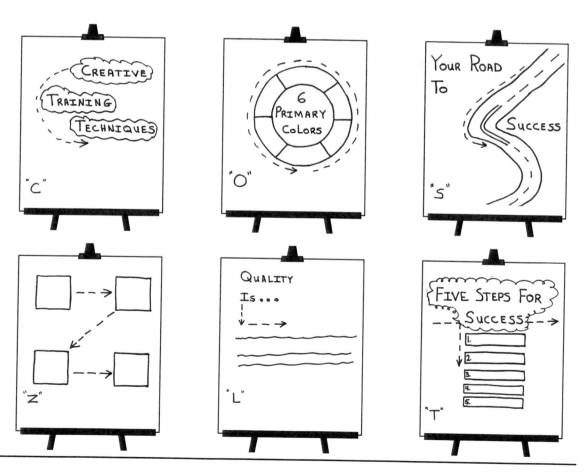

LAYOUT IMPORTANCE OF BALANCE

The further an image (or word) appears from the center of your page, the more it seems to draw attention in that direction. There are two common approaches for displaying your material on a page: *formal balance* and *informal balance*.

Formal Balance

Formal balance means that items are equally matched or displayed in a symmetrical pattern so that a participant's attention is not pulled in one direction or the other.

Note How the Text Is Centered with Equivalent Sized Images on Either Side. These Images Complement and "Bracket" the Text Forming a "Formal Balance."

Informal Balance

Informal balance means that the displayed objects are asymmetrical or unequal in size, shape, or pattern. This technique attracts attention to one area or another and can add contrast. Care must be given not to detract from your intended objective by making the informal balance too extreme.

Note How This Chart Has Only One Image with No Other Complementing Graphic on the Opposite Side of the Page. This Can Cause the Reader's Eye to Be Drawn Away from the Text and to the Side of the Page. The Result Is an "Informal Balance."

BRIGHT IDEA

To get the feel of formal and informal balance and what the concepts look like on your flip chart, draw and cut out a variety of images and shapes that you may want to use now and in the future (smile faces, boxes, rectangles, simple people figures, or whatever). Spray the cutouts with artist's adhesive (see *Appendix* C), then practice placing them at various locations on your page. Next, try adding some lettering and move your images around.

Text should be evenly spaced and start at the same position on each page. To maintain visual balance, consider leaving the same margin on all sides of the text—for example, 3 inches (7.5 cm) from the top and bottom edges of the paper and 3 inches (7.5 cm) from the left and right edges. When adding graphics, keep their size in proportion to the rest of the information shown.

LAYOUT OF TEXT-ONLY FLIP CHARTS

Whenever possible, text-only flip charts should also be arranged in the letter patterns described above. Another cardinal rule is: "Leave plenty of white space." Create a border of white space of at least 2 inches (5 cm) on the top, bottom, and sides. Also, leave 1 inch (2.5 cm) or more of white space between lines. Your chart will have a cleaner, more professional appearance and help participants distinguish between thoughts or ideas.

In addition, try to balance words with a fairly equal amount of space on either side. With lists of items consisting of only one to three words, you may want to center each line on the page. Also, leave plenty of blank space in the upper corners for writing presentation notes to yourself (in small print that only you can see.) Never "crowd" information (text or graphics) on the page.

Good Layout   **Bad Layout**

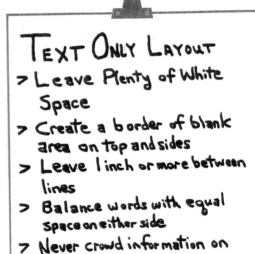

Note the Amount of White Space Left on the Page.

Note the Number and Placment of Words. Suggested Techniques Being Described by the Image Are Being Ignored.

Many presenters or meeting facilitators list information in vertical columns in order to show comparisons or related information. This is a good technique, provided the display is limited to three columns per page—to make reading easier and to present a more professional look. If you are partial to columns, you may want to consider distributing the information as a handout as well. This may help people in the back from having to strain to read the text.

Two columns are the maximum that I find to be effective, unless I'm simply listing single words or terms under each column. Sentences or lines of text under columns definitely push the limits of effectiveness and challenge the reader.

POSITIONING TITLES

As you visualize your flip chart layout, consider where to position your title line to add impact. It does not have to be at the top of the page. For variety, you can move the title lines around on the page a bit without sacrificing effectiveness. As before, take out a few sheets of paper and play with positioning. Write out several titles, spray them with artist's adhesive, and try various locations on the page. The following images offer a couple of possibilities.

Examples of Title Placement Layouts

EACH WORD SHOULD BE LEGIBLE FROM THE BACK OF THE ROOM

To ensure that those at the far reaches of your room can read your text, be conscious of where you position your flip chart easel—and keep the layout simple. Follow the suggestions outlined in this section and avoid "data dump." Too much information makes reading difficult or impossible and can frustrate or anger participants who cannot read what you have written. Remember that your goal in using a flip chart is to highlight key words and concepts, not show your entire presentation outline on paper. Focus on enhancing the clarity of your message and reinforcing your presentation.

At one business presentation I attended recently, I am convinced that the speaker did everything she could to make the information unreadable. There were no title lines, and numbers were haphazardly spread around the page. The presenter added more numbers in the small margins as she spoke and she selected only a red marker even though she had a box of assorted colors to choose from.

I kept telling myself, "Bob, don't be so critical just because you know the 'rules' of flip charting." However, after the meeting, I asked another participant what she thought of the marathon meeting we'd just attended. Her reaction was, "I have a headache from looking at all those numbers and trying to follow the meaning."

THE SIX TO EIGHT RULE

One of the more common mistakes that presenters and facilitators make with flip charts is to jam too much information on a page. This cluttered look is typically ineffective and frustrating for the reader. As with overhead transparencies, I recommend limiting the number of lines per flip chart page. A good rule of thumb is to write six to eight words per line, using letters 2 to 3 inches (5–7.5 cm) high; for your title line, use 4-inch (10-cm) letters. Maintain a maximum of six to eight lines of text per page (including the title line).

There are three good reasons for limiting the amount of information you put on each line and page:

1. Aesthetically it looks better, since you eliminate unnecessary detail and clutter.

2. It aids the visual flow across the page, since participants do not have to read as many words and can now focus their attention on what you are saying.

3. Research shows that the human brain can effectively retain seven units or chunks of information (plus or minus two) in short-term memory.[*]

[*]G. A. Miller, "The Magical Number of Seven, Plus or Minus Two: Some Limits on Our Capacity for Processing Information," *Psychology Review*, 63 (1956), pp. 81–97.

As with any rule, there are going to be exceptions. For example, if you are writing a long string of items or capturing ideas presented from participants, it is obvious that your list will run on to a subsequent page. In such instances, you might go to the bottom of the page, tear it off, and have someone tape it high enough on the wall so you can create a continuous list. You can then move on to the next page and, once finished, tape the second page at the bottom of the first.

HOW TO WRITE ON THE BOTTOM OF A FLIP CHART PAGE

Have you ever seen someone try to write at the bottom of a flip chart page? It's hard! Some people get very creative in their approach while trying not to look ridiculous. Let me first say that unless you're doing a continuation page, as indicated in the last section, you may want to leave the bottom third of the page blank. Otherwise, participants who have to look over other people's heads may not be able to see everything you have written.

If you must write on the bottom portion, here are some options:

- Kneel down in front of the easel for easy access. The drawback to this techniques for female presenters wearing dresses is obvious. Also, depending on your physical condition—especially if you have a knee or back problem—you may have difficulty getting up gracefully (or at all).

- Tip the easel away from you as you write. This may be a challenge, depending on the weight and construction of the easel and your own physical dexterity.

- Lean forward at the waist and carefully print your words. If nothing else, the pose provides an interesting perspective for your audience!

- Pull a chair over to the easel and sit while writing. Although this position may be comfortable, it will take a bit of coordination for you to move the furniture.

- Pull the bottom edge of the page up toward you and write while holding it. If you are like me, you will find that your handwriting suffers along with your ability to write consistently and in a straight line when using this method.

- Slide the edge of the page up the easel and use the pad and easel for support as you write. This may be one of the better techniques for readability; however, it will still take some coordination as you slide, bend, and write.

My suggestion—leave the bottom third blank!

USING COLOR

To add variety and visual perspective and to emphasize key words or concepts, try alternating ink colors between ideas or text lines. (See Chapter 3, on spicing up your flip charts with graphics for advanced ideas.) My basic advice when using colors is to do so judiciously. Don't try to capture the entire color spectrum on a single chart. A rainbow presentation can appear cumbersome and confusing. It also can be distracting as you locate, cap, and uncap a variety of different markers. By the same token, using just one color is less effective than using two or three. Usually, two to three complementary colors are best. A simple way to create contrast is to add bullets to your text using a different-colored marker.

LIMIT AND COMPRESS THE INFORMATION ON EACH PAGE

Putting just one idea or concept on a page helps participants follow your presentation. When you complicate the page with too many facts or unrelated details, efficiency is often lost. This is especially true when you are showing columns of numbers. Limit yourself to 25 to 35 individual numbers on the page. If you have a lot of information, I suggest that you summarize it on your flip chart, then distribute a handout with the details. Simpler is better with flip charts.

Bad Example   **Good Example**

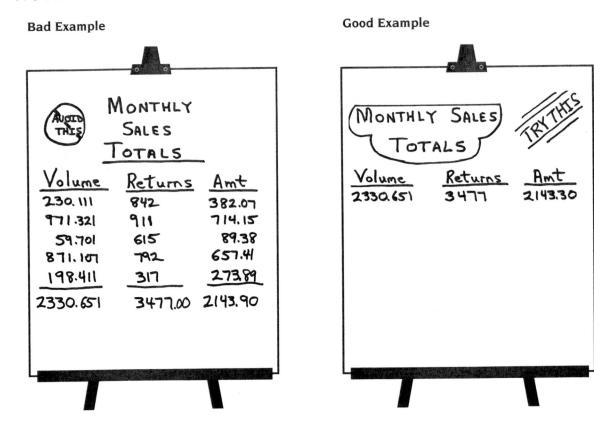

Save space by using numerical digits, symbols, abbreviations, and other devices when possible, but be consistent in your application—use the same spelling, symbol, or format throughout the presentation. Here are a few examples:

- Instead of the word *dollar*, write $.
- For the word *percent*, use %.
- Instead of the word *with*, try *w*.
- Instead of *without*, try *w/o*.
- Use numbers to replace words—for example, write 2 instead of *to* and 4 instead of *for*.

To get more information onto lines of text, shorten sentences by using acronyms, numbers, and abbreviations instead of complete words. Another option is to use only key words. When you take these shortcuts, make sure that the symbols you choose are known to participants. If not, explain your shorthand when you first introduce it to the group.

There are two basic approaches to abbreviating the words in a sentence:

- Leave out vowels. For example, write *mngt* for *management* or *cnslt* for *consult*.

- Shorten words. Abbreviate them by leaving off part of the letters. For example, write *manage.* for *management* or *consult.* for *consultant*. The only problem with this technique is that abbreviated words that are complete words in themselves (such as the examples above) can be confusing.

As mentioned, you can also use acronyms (new words formed by using only the first letters of other words), numbers, or key words to reduce the number of items on your flip charts.

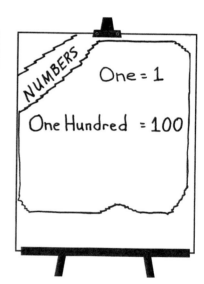

BRIGHT IDEA

To add a bit of variety, create an acronym from the first letter of each word in a series of words or phrases, then spell out the acronym down the left side of the flip chart page, writing just the first letter of each word. For example, HOMES is an acronym for the Great Lakes of the United States (Huron, Ontario, Michigan, Erie, and Superior). ADDIE stands for the instructional systems design model (assess, design, develop, implement, and evaluate). As you go through the list and introduce the word or concept represented by each letter, fill in the remainder of the word. Acronym lists are a variation of the revelation technique explained elsewhere in this book.

When you are writing responses from participants, be careful not to substitute words for the ideas they offer. You may inadvertently change their intended meaning or offend them by discounting what they say as your paraphrase. If you want to modify what a participant says, ask for permission. This is awkward, however, since some people may agree, and still feel offended that you didn't use *their* idea or word. They may even stop contributing. It is better to ask permission than to assume a change is all right. It is even better to use *their* word.

To communicate complex processes or concepts, you may want to use charts or graphs. Appropriate themes for this approach are percentages, time distributions, frequencies, and relationships among items.

Percentages

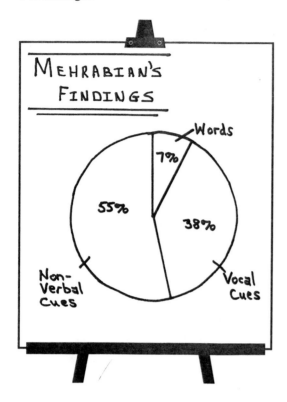

Time

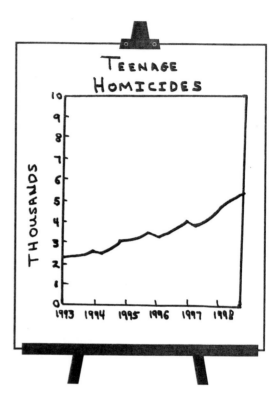

Frequency

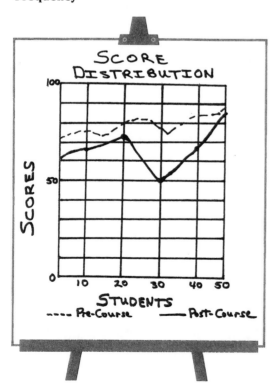

Relationship

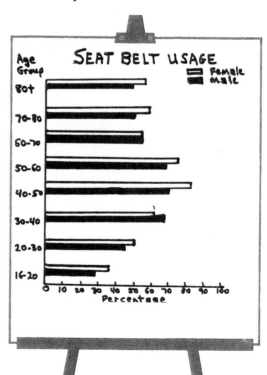

HOW TO HIDE YOUR MISTAKES

You do not have to throw away a page or obliterate a word with a marker when you make a spelling or grammatical error on prepared flip charts. You have a variety of options for correcting errors or misspelled words on the spot. One technique is to quickly cut out a piece of blank flip chart paper large enough to cover the error and tape it over the mistake. You're now ready to continue drawing, and the correction will not be noticeable to most people in the room.

Here is a variation if you make a mistake while preparing a fancy flip chart for a presentation. Place a blank sheet of flip chart paper over the mistake you've made. Using an Exacto knife or single-edged razor blade, cut out the misspelled word through the blank page. You now have a blank section exactly the same size as the section where the misspelled word was earlier. Place the blank piece into the opening on your original sheet and tape it from the rear. Even the people in the front row will have trouble seeing that the correction was made.

Another option is to buy a package of large white shipping labels (you can even use white name tags) and paste one or more over the error. The downside of this technique is that the color probably will not match your flip chart paper. Your can also purchase a wide roll of white correction tape from an art or office supply store. Simply tape over the area and continue to write. Again, if you are a stickler for matching color, this solution may not work for you.

Finally, there is a unique product called Spray Mark Over, typically used in warehouses to spray over errors or lettering on cardboard boxes. (See Appendix C.) After you spray, you can write over the patch. (As with any aerosol product, use only in well-ventilated areas and away from people with allergies and respiratory conditions.) The spray comes in white and tan, but it may not exactly match your paper color or look as professional as some of the other techniques discussed. Unless you're using rolls of butcher paper or white flip chart pads for your writing surface, this spray technique may not work for you.

Chapter 2

WRITING WELL ON A FLIP CHART—EVEN IF YOU HAVE POOR HANDWRITING

WRITING IN A STRAIGHT LINE

Writing in a straight line is a challenge for many people. For a polished look that aids reading and saves paper, your goal should be to write across the pages in a level horizontal line. If you have difficulty writing straight, one option is to use flip chart paper with predrawn lines or grids. You can also draw faint lines on the pages with a yardstick and pencil at 3-inch to 5-inch (7.5–12.5 cm) intervals. Instead of adding one line at a time to create a predrawn chart, go to a school supply store and ask for a little device that teachers use to draw lines on a chalkboard. (See Appendix C.) These wooden-handled tools have six metal "fingers," each of which can hold a pencil. Load your sharpened pencils and away you go, drawing six straight lines at a stroke.

The trick to writing in a straight line—if you're not using ruled paper, is to position yourself properly in relation to the flip chart easel. If you are right-handed, stand just off center to the left of your easel, as you face it (left-handers, stand to the right as you face the easel). Try to move as far to the side as you can so that you will not block the reader's view as you write. From your off-center location, you should be able to write all the way across

Linemaker for Chalkboards

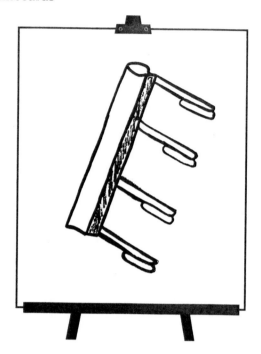

the page without moving, provided your arms are long enough. We have all witnessed (or been prey to) the "falling sentence syndrome," in which the written lines of text arch from a high point downward on the page. The trick is to write rapidly and not talk as you do so: Turn (to the easel), write (concentrating on keeping your lines straight), turn (to your audience), point (at what you wrote), and talk.

WRITING LEGIBLY

I have never been accused of having legible handwriting. Actually, I have been advised to improve many times. My first-grade teacher, Ms. Grace Pelaez, noted on my report card, "Robert must continue to try harder to do nice, neat written work." Try as I might, it's still a struggle! However, when flip-charting, I have found the solution to be planning, repetition, practice, and taking the time to go slow.

Falling Sentence Syndrome

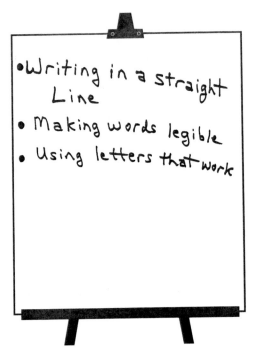

The first element—*planning*—comes from thinking ahead to allow myself enough time to write the words correctly and legibly. When preparing pages in advance, I try to give myself as much time as needed to do the job correctly. I do my charts days in advance to cover the possibility that an error, unforeseen event, or interruption might occur. Unless a client calls me the day ahead to schedule a meeting, I never wait until the night before a presentation to get started. I also build enough time into my presentation schedule for soliciting, flip-charting, and discussing participant comments.

The second element—*repetition*—refers to using the same font styles throughout a series of flip chart pages for a program. I typically use block lettering when writing in class and when adding text lines to predrawn charts. However, for cover or introductory pages designed for a program, I get a bit more adventuresome and try fancy, overlapping, italic, or billowing styles.

The third element—*practice*—comes into play when I lay out my preplanned pages on a writing tablet first, then copy them onto a flip chart pad. Also, after using similar fonts and techniques for more than 26 years of presenting and speaking, I have discovered what works and doesn't for me.

The final element—*going slow*—is easier said than done. But when I rush, my handwriting suffers. So I take the time I need.

Sizing Titles and Text

For ease of reading, you should leave appropriate spacing between lines of text. As discussed earlier, the more white space you provide, the easier it is to follow your presentation. Here are some general considerations related to size:

- If your letters are 2 inches (5 cm) high, leave approximately 1 inch (2.5 cm) between lines; otherwise the lines can appear to merge from a distance.

- Generally, use capital letters for title lines only. Use a combination of uppercase and lowercase lettering for text lines, as in most printed texts.

- As a rule, lettering that is 1/2 inch (1.25 cm) high is visible from 16 to 18 feet (4.5–5.5 m) for someone with average sight. Every 1/4 inch (.65 cm) adds approximately another 8 feet (2.5 m) of visibility. Anything beyond 50 to 60 feet (15–18 m) can be difficult to read. In these cases, try handouts, overhead projection, or other thechniques.

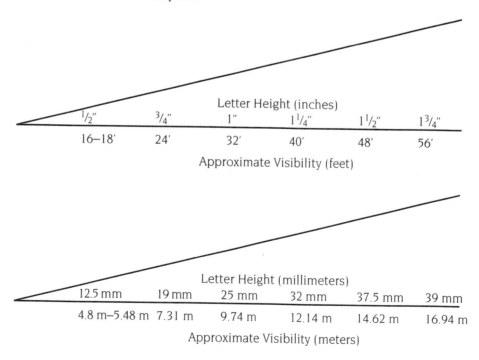

Letter Height (inches)					
1/2"	3/4"	1"	1 1/4"	1 1/2"	1 3/4"
16–18'	24'	32'	40'	48'	56'

Approximate Visibility (feet)

Letter Height (millimeters)					
12.5 mm	19 mm	25 mm	32 mm	37.5 mm	39 mm
4.8 m–5.48 m	7.31 m	9.74 m	12.14 m	14.62 m	16.94 m

Approximate Visibility (meters)

Consistency

When facilitating train-the-trainer programs, I stress the need for consistency to my attendees. Their ability to create a "look" and carry it throughout their programs is important to their success and what their participants will learn.

To ensure that your printing looks the same throughout your presentation, use the same style, size, and angle for your letters. Maintaining the same amount of distance between letters and lines as you write is also important and can greatly aid appearance and readability. In addition, as you progress through a series of pages related to the same topic and theme, repeat the color patterns and bullets. For example, if you use stars on page 1 along with black ink for the first, third, and fifth lines and then blue ink for the second, fourth, and sixth lines, follow the same pattern on page 2. Repetition helps you and your participants follow the theme. Also, when you refer back to pages posted on the wall, participants can quickly figure out what relates to what.

As with any other aspect of presenting your message well to groups, the key to writing consistently on flip charts is practice!

CREATIVE USE OF FONTS

Creative fonts, bullets, underlines, and other devices are effective when they are not overused. Deviating occasionally from your basic black printed lettering, especially with creative font variations or graphics, is a great way to add flair or emphasis to your presentation. Just don't get so caught up with drawing entertaining objects or fonts that you steer attention away from your program message.

There are dozens of options for fancy font styles in typical desktop publishing programs today. Microsoft Word has an entire section of creative and artistically designed font patterns. Such designs can easily be imitated with a little practice or can be printed, enlarged, traced, cut out, colored, and attached to your flip chart. As with any other strategy discussed in this book, practice is the key to creating lettering that will advance your message. The following images show several examples of what I mean.

Block Letters

I typically use block letters such as those below, rather than cursive letters or custom, elaborate, and/or intricate font types. That does not mean that occasionally I don't use fancier styles to emphasize a point or create an eye-catching cover page or title line. Block letters, however, aid participant readability and comprehension.

Generally, I draw my letters freehand. You can do likewise, or you can purchase a commercial lettering stencil from a school, office, department, or art supply store. The important thing is that your end result adds value to your presentation. To find your own comfort level or style, experiment with a variety of letter shapes and thicknesses. Once you find a couple you like, practice drawing and using them regularly.

A B C D E F G H I J K L M
N O P Q R S T U V W X Y Z
a b c d e f g h i j k l m
n o p q r s t u v w x y z
1 2 3 4 5 6 7 8 9 0

 Practice Your Skills. Let's see how good your block letters look. Take out several sheets of notepaper and write each of the block letters and numbers above five times. Make each character at least 1 inch (2.54 cm) high.

Cursive Letters

Shadowed or cursive fonts are all right for adding emphasis or possibly as title lines. However, avoid using them for text lines, since they may begin to run together as the distance between the flip chart and participants increases.

Shaded or Artistic Fonts

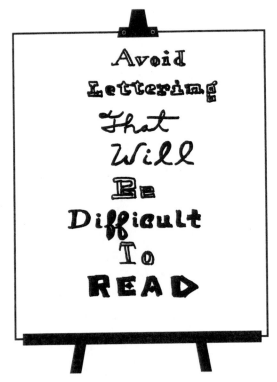

Practice Your Skills. Take out several sheets of lined notepaper and practice writing the cursive alphabet five times. Make each letter 1 inch (2.54 cm) high.

Billowing Letters

Billowing fonts appear "fluffy" like clouds and can add a softer, less formal look to your flip chart pages.

Billowing Letters

Practice Your Skills. Take out several sheets of lined paper and practice writing the billowing letter alphabet five times. Make each letter 1 inch (2.54 cm) high.

Overlapping Letters

Although overlapping letters are good for adding emphasis or highlighting a cover sheet word or title line, they can be difficult to read, especially from a distance.

Overlapping Letters

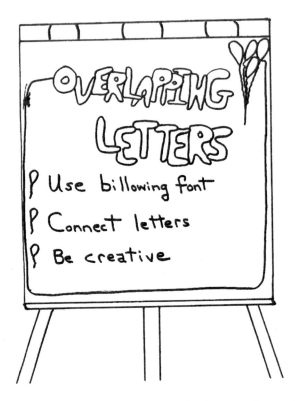

 Practice Your Skills. Take out several sheets of lined paper and practice writing the overlapping letter alphabet five times. Make each letter 1 inch (2.54 cm) high.

Fancy Letters

To add a more formal or classy look, you may want to consider using fancy letters (especially ones with serifs) from the font library of your word processing program.

A	B	C	D	E	F	G	H	I	J	K	L	M
N	O	P	Q	R	S	T	U	V	W	X	Y	Z
a	b	c	d	e	f	g	h	i	j	k	l	m
n	o	p	q	r	s	t	u	v	w	x	y	z
1	2	3	4	5	6	7	8	9	0			

Practice Your Skills. Practice writing the fancy letter alphabet five times. Make each letter 1 inch (2.54 cm) high.

Italic Letters

You can add the impression of italicized lettering by slanting your letters to the right. An easy way to draw italicized letters is to use lined paper, lay your pad flat, then turn it at a 30° angle to the right (or left, depending on which hand you write with). Now write your letters straight up and down toward what would normally be the top direction of your page—instant italics!

Italics

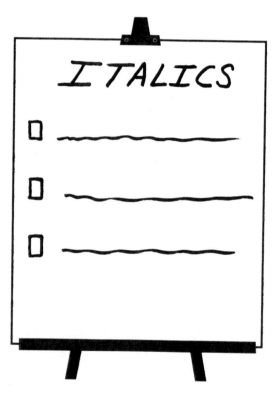

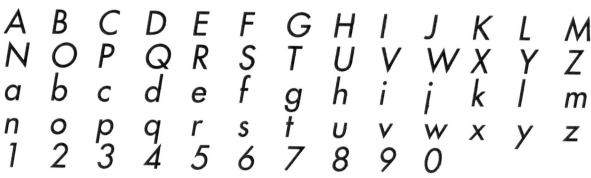

Practice Your Skills. Take out several sheets of lined paper and practice writing the italic letter alphabet five times. Make each letter 1 inch (appx 2.54cm) high.

CREATIVE IDEAS FOR BULLETS

Bullets (not the type with gunpowder!) can be very helpful for indicating the start of a new thought, idea, or concept on your page. Bullets are especially effective when you use designs related to your presentation theme. For example, if you are making a presentation on using audiovisual aids as training tools, you can use miniature flip chart easels, overhead projectors, audiotapes or videocassettes as bullets. You can also use circles, squares, or other geometric shapes. If you do not want to draw your own bullets, yet wish to use these symbols on your flip charts, you have two good choices. You can buy either large colored adhesive dots or rolls of large colored smile-face stickers from an office supply store. (See the creative presentation resources in Appendix C.) You can then alternate the colors between points. These options help eliminate the confusion that some facilitators and trainers encounter in trying to keep their bullet size consistent and using the right colored marker.

To prevent distraction, I try to limit the size of bullets to one-half the height of the lettering that follows them. I also try to consistently use the same shape throughout a series of pages that cover a single issue. Switching to a different bullet could be a misleading (nonverbal) signal that I have closed one topic and am moving to another one. In a given session, I normally use only two or three different bullet shapes. Too much variety can distract me and my participants.

In addition, when bulleting subpoints, I usually indent a bit more than I do for key items. This helps viewers identify what is more important and aids readability. It also looks prettier! One final thought related to bullets: By using them instead of numbers or letters, you remove the mindset that an item numbered 1 is more important than one numbered 4 or that point A is more crucial than point C. Numbers and letters tend to suggest an order, priority, or sequence. Bullets simply indicate a new concept or idea and mark their place on the page. (See Appendix A for examples of bullet shapes.) Note: The "Italics" graphic on page 29 shows how a bullet might appear.

CREATIVE IDEAS FOR UNDERLINING

Underlining is a simple way of emphasizing key words or ideas on your pages. However, instead of simply drawing a plain line under your text, use a little creativity. Try holding two different-colored markers in one hand so that the points are parallel. Now draw a dual colored line under your text! Look over the section on colors in Chapter 3 before rushing off to draw your lines. Some colors complement one another; others do the opposite.

To carry the idea of colored lines one step further, pick up a few metallic ink markers at an art supply store. Get the widest-tipped markers available. You can now add some real sparkle to your charts. Neon-colored markers also provide an exciting change from the normal color spectrum. There are many variations of the simple underline that can draw attention to a specific area of your page. Here are a few more.

Creative Underlining

Chapter 3

SPICING UP YOUR FLIP CHARTS WITH GRAPHICS— EVEN IF YOU CAN'T DRAW

I have always been envious of trainers and presenters who can spontaneously create a visual to match their message and seem to have an endless repertoire of graphic images. That is because I'm a left-brain thinker (more analytical than artistic), and for me to come up with images or envision a theme on the spot is a stretch. To compensate I have built a collection of images over the years that I have practiced drawing and can call upon at will. (See Appendix A.) The importance of graphics is one of the main reasons I wrote this book—to help me and the people in my *Presentation Pizzazz* and Flip Chart Magic workshops engage in more creative flip charting.

Every presentation can benefit from appealing graphics. According to the 3M Company of St. Paul, Minnesota, there are five objectives for which a visual aid is particularly helpful:

1. To grab attention at the start of a session, (e.g., through a catchy cartoon, drawing, or quote).

2. To emphasize key points, such as session objectives or major issues.

3. To present statistical data using an easily understood format, such as a pie chart or bar graph.

4. To compare data being presented, such as sales or profit forecasts.

5. To illustrate an item that is either too big or too small to display adequately, such as a piece of equipment.

Once you know you need one or more graphics for your presentation, you have two choices: Draw it yourself or find a sample and copy it. This book will help you do both. This chapter provides several opportunities for you to practice simple graphics. I present an assortment of common business graphics that you are encouraged to copy from.

ADDING GRAPHICS

Simple graphic images are an easy way to break the monotony of rows of words on a page. By drawing a small figure or symbol as you prepare pages in advance, or adding a symbol as you write down participants' comments, you can highlight, draw attention, entertain, or emphasize some aspect of your presentation. By bringing in artwork, you can add color and variety while giving a visual introduction to your new topic.*

There are literally thousands of images from which you can choose. Go to any art store or library, thumb through the phone company yellow pages, or look in "junk mail" advertisements you receive. Check through software graphics packages, children's coloring books, or any other source you can think of. Graphics are everywhere! For years, I've cut out small images that I liked and tossed them into a "clip art" file in my drawer. Now, whenever I need an idea for an image I look there first. There is now an HR image software on the market. (See the creative presentation resources in Appendix C for more information.)

When choosing your graphic images, keep these points in mind:

1. Be creative and humorous, and utilize your imagination to develop a program with a dash of flair.

2. Use bold, broad-line pictures that can be seen from a distance of at least 30 feet (9 m). Also, avoid complex, detail-oriented images that may blur at a distance—simpler is better. Line art

*I'm always interested in getting your feedback on creative ways you have incorporated the images in your presentations. My contact information is included in the Introduction to this book. Send me a picture or sketch of your masterpiece, and I'll respond with a present you can use to spark up your presentations.

is usually the safest. You can always give participants a hand-out of your charts later to provide details.

3. Learn to create very simple characters and objects. Start with stick figure or "people" shapes. Again, Part IV provides many predrawn images you can copy and use. A list of materials and training programs to help get you started appears in Appendix C.

Sample Stick Figures

4. Choose your images objectively and wisely. Remember, not every picture evokes the same thoughts or feelings for all viewers. Choose more generic graphics that tend to have the same meaning to virtually all viewers, and avoid controversial social, religious, or political images that may cause contentious feelings. Also, keep in mind that when your audience members are from a variety of countries, cultural interpretations may vary.

5. Select images that complement your written text or add value to the page. Do not make the mistake of using an image just to fill empty space.

6. Don't worry if you lack the talent of a Rembrandt or Picasso. As long as your images are recognizable, they serve their purpose.

To get you thinking, I've drawn a few basic images to help:

Generic Graphic Images

Practice Your Skills. Drawing simple graphic images or cartoon figures is not as difficult as you may think. To get started, find a couple of basic images you like (possibly from one of the sources listed earlier or some of the samples drawn above). Next, take some paper and a pencil and start drawing an image as you look at it. Continue to draw the image until you feel you have memorized it. Once you reach that level, put the original and what you have drawn away and try to capture the image freehand. Compare your new drawing with the original. How did you do? If you mastered the first image, choose another and repeat the process. Keep a notebook of simple images you have learned how to draw.

PREDRAW YOUR GRAPHICS

Here's another little secret I've learned over the years. To help create the appearance of being a talented artist when you add graphics in front of a group, predraw your title lines and graphics before a session begins. Use a pencil to very lightly trace an outline of a geometric shape (circle, triangle, square, etc.), simple diagram, flow chart, model, image, or picture on the page. Later, when you are ready to add words or collect participant input, flip to the page and trace the image quickly with the broad edge of your marker. Voilà—instant artist! Viewers are impressed, you add a splash of excitement, and you will likely feel better about the end result.

BRIGHT IDEA

Keep in mind that the artwork should complement and reinforce the text. Always position information and graphics carefully. For example, if you have a stick figure person or graphic image on the chart, make sure that it is facing or looking in the direction of the words. This subtle technique is more visually appealing. Also, subconsciously, the participant's attention follows the direction of your images.

Graphic Image Positioning

USE ICONS AS BULLETS

Sample Bulleted Icons

"Icon bullets" add visual intensity or color, and draw attention to your message. These icons can be duplicated in handout materials as a way to connect the narrative and printed data. For example, for a telemarketing presentation, you might use small telephone receivers as bullets on flip charts and related handouts. For my supervisory workshop entitled *Working Effectively with Others*, I use the scales of justice, often associated with courts and lawyers, on flip charts, in marketing materials, and on handouts. Since the workshop deals with creating a positive work environment and understanding various employment laws, this graphic image subconsciously sends a message that legal issues are associated with the program. (See the sample icons in Appendix A.)

To enhance a title line or key concept, you can surround it with icons of clouds, boxes, explosions, banners, geometric figures, stars, arrows, or other symbols.

Sample Shapes

BRIGHT IDEA

Here's a technique I saw a friend of mine use many years ago. He went to a print supplier and had rubber stamps made with 1-inch (2.54 cm) images of stars, smile faces, squares, solid circles, and triangles. Today, you can get some of these same stamp images off the shelf in an office supply store. You may even be able to get self-inking stamps in a variety of colors. These print up quickly and are great for the artistically challenged who want to add bullets to their flip charts. If you or your company is the original author of a logo, symbol, or icon, you can provide a sample of the graphic drawing to an office or craft supply house. The store can prepare a rubber stamp in your desired size within a few days for a minimal expense—usually less than $25. You can order a variety of sizes and shapes (e.g., a company logo, graphic images, state seals and flags) to suit your needs.

USING COLOR

Color can enhance your visual message when used appropriately and can have the opposite effect when used improperly. Color can be used to give emphasis, achieve harmony in an image, connect concepts, or guide a viewer's eye through a page of information or images. Research also shows that most people prefer color to a bland white background with black lettering. Emphasizing key points with color can be vital to getting your information across to viewers, especially in the third hour of the program and onward, when attention spans grow short. If participant attention is waning and distractions are occurring, colored highlights (especially used for the first time in the presentation) can bring the subject back into focus.

The key to success when using color is to be conservative. More than three colors can make a page appear busy and can distract or confuse your viewer. When combining, try to use colors that are related and that appear next to each other on the color wheel. Colors opposite each other on the wheel also go well together and add a degree of contrast. Red, orange, and yellow are warm colors that pull attention or seem to leap off the page. Violet, blue, and green are cool colors that provide good background in visuals.

Color Wheel

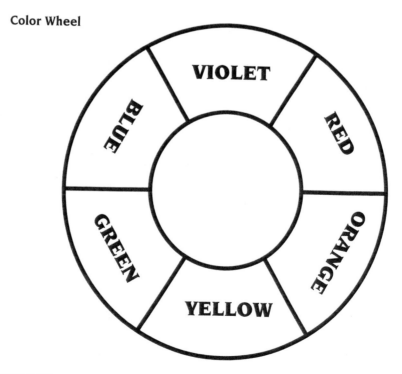

A creative approach for giving variety to your pages is to alternate marker colors from one idea to the next. For example, you might use black, blue, and dark green, in that order. You can then use red to write or underline key words or concepts you wish to emphasize.

A caution on the color red. I advise against using it to print your entire page. The reason is that it may be hard to read from a distance, and some people have trouble seeing shades of red. Orange, yellow, and pastel colors are nice to look at; however, they should be used only to add highlights or a splash of color in artwork, borders, or other graphic devices. These colors are extremely difficult to see in low light and from a distance.

One technique I use to help carry a theme or continue the process flow is to coordinate the use of colors throughout the series of pages. For example, if my title line on the front page is black encased in an orange "cloud," I use the same color scheme on subsequent related pages. As with the technique of using similar bullets this approach nonverbally connects information and adds fast referral later on during reviews. It also helps me keep track of where I am when someone sidetracks the discussion as I flip-chart an issue or facilitate a meeting.

THE EMOTION OF COLOR

Understanding the emotions evoked by certain colors will help you choose the right ones for your presentations. For example, bright, "hot," or neon colors attract more attention and can excite, stimulate, raise emotions, and grab attention better than "cool," dark colors. On the other hand, cooler colors can relax, soothe, or calm those looking at them.

Colors can be used to draw upon specific emotions or send nonverbal messages. This concept has been used extensively in marketing for years. The following list shows how the concept works.

Color	Emotion/Message
Red	Stimulates and evokes excitement, passion, power, energy, anger, and intensity. Also, can indicate "stop," negativity, financial trouble, or shortage.

Color	Emotion/Message
Yellow	Indicates caution, warmth, mellowness, positive meaning, optimism, and cheerfulness. It can also stimulate thinking and visioning.
Dark blue	Depending on shade, can relax, soothe, indicate maturity, and evoke trust, tranquility, or peace.
Light blue	Cool, youthful, or masculine image can be projected.
Purple	Projects assertiveness or boldness, youthfulness, and contemporary image. Often used as a sign of royalty, richness, spirituality, or power.
Orange	Can indicate high energy or enthusiasm. Has emotional power and sometimes stimulates positive thinking. Organic image can result.
Brown	An earth tone that creates a feeling of security, wholesomeness, strength, support, and lack of pretentiousness.
Green	Evokes nature, productivity, positive image, moving forward or "go," comforting, growth, financial success, or prosperity. Also, can give a feeling of balance.
Gold/Silver	Illustrates prestige, status, wealth, elegance, or conservative image.
Pink	Projects youthful, feminine, or warm image.
White	Typically used to illustrate purity, cleanliness, honesty, or wholesomeness; enhances colors used and provides visual relaxation.
Black	Represents lack of color. Creates sense of independence, completeness, and solidarity. Often used to indicate financial success, death, seriousness, or heaviness of situation.

ADDING BORDERS

I use borders in a variety of patterns and shapes to segment information. Their design can range from simple combinations of colored lines (single, double, or a combination) to the various themed styles available in graphics software.

You can also use borders related to your program themes to add creativity. For example, if your topic is expanding your international sales into a new foreign market, you might border the page, or separate sections of data, with that nation's flag or one of its famous landmarks.

Sample Borders

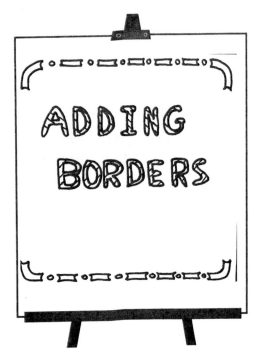

TRACING IMAGES

You say you're still creatively challenged? Then cheat! If you want to use a graphic image on your flip chart that needs to be larger than ones created and printed from a computer, simply copy or print the image onto a transparency. Then, using an overhead projector, project the image onto the flip chart page, and trace it. You can enlarge the image by moving the paper farther away from the projector or shrink it by moving closer.

Tracing Images from an Overhead Projector

BRIGHT IDEA

To add graphic shapes to your pages, visit the art, craft, or department stores in your area. There are literally hundreds of items used by artists and craft enthusiasts that can serve as guides for drawing flip chart images to enhance your presentation. For example, plastic or wooden figures in the shape of flowers, clothing, furniture, or equipment can become templates for graphic icons or images. Simply put the figure on an overhead projector, project the image onto your flip chart paper, and trace. A word of caution: If the object being projected is hard, place a piece of clear transparency film or document protector under it to prevent scratching the glass surface.

Pantograph

Another way to trace items from a page to your flip chart pad is to use an artist's pantograph (available at any art store). Remember that little adjustable gate-like device many of us used as kids? One end has a point for tracing along the lines of an image; the other holds a pencil that is positioned on a blank page. As you follow the lines on the original image with one end of the pantograph, a copy is made simultaneously on the blank paper at the other, penciled end. Images can be enlarged or reduced, but not copied at the exact size. (See resources in Appendix C.)

Pantograph

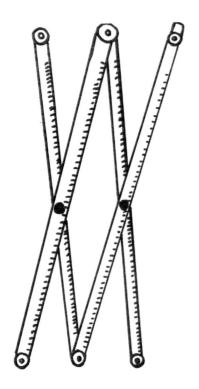

Projection Device

A third option for tracing an image is to purchase a projection device used by graphic design artists. This handy tool can be used to enlarge projected images onto your flip chart page so you can copy them. There are a couple of drawbacks, however. The first is that the area that can be viewed and projected is only about 7" × 7" (17.78 × 17.78 cm). Also, some of the projector models get a bit warm after extended use and may damage a plastic icon or coated image, such as a photograph or transparency film.

On the positive side, these small projectors can be used without an overhead device. They are on the low price end, averaging below $100, and in some cases can enlarge up to 3000 percent or reduce down to 70 percent of the original image.

DRAWING PERFECT CIRCLES

Need to draw large, evenly shaped circles? There are several options. For example, you can always use the lid of a large plastic bowl. On the other hand, you can head for your art or school supply store and ask for a commercial compass. The old-fashioned chalkboard compass can be made narrow or wide to draw circles of various dimensions. Two alternatives for creating perfect circles are the clip compass and the flip chart compass.

Chalkboard Compass

The chalkboard compass is usually made of wood and is used on dry erase and chalkboards. You can modify it for use on flip charts. (See the Where to Find Flip Charts Accessories and Resources in Appendix C.)

Clip Compass

The clip compass is a smaller device for drawing circles up to 9 inches (22.86 cm). It has a spring-loaded clip for holding a marker, crayon, pencil, or cutting knife. Position it on your paper, rotate, and you get a perfect circle each time.

Flip Chart Compass

The flip chart compass is actually a multipurpose drawing tool that has been modified for use with flip charts. It functions as a compass, protractor, straight edge, angle template, and horizontal ruler. By inserting a marker in one end and positioning it on your paper, you can again create perfect circles. (See Appendix C.)

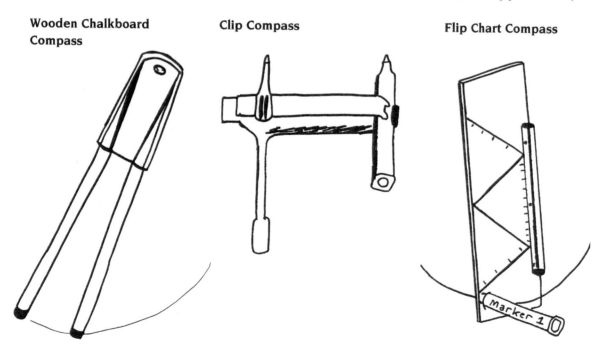

Wooden Chalkboard Compass   **Clip Compass**   **Flip Chart Compass**

BRIGHT IDEA

Need a large circle for an early-morning program and the stores are all closed? Alternatives to commercial compasses, for drawing circles of various sizes, are standard wooden rulers or yardsticks. Simply drill small holes at incremental points on the ruler and place it over your paper. Next, place a stickpin through the first hole in the ruler to secure it to the point you wish to be the center of your circle. Then slip the point of a pencil through the hole at the size of the circle you desire (e.g., 6 inches, or 15.24 cm). Slide the ruler around in a fluid motion to draw your circle.

ATTACHING ITEMS TO FLIP CHARTS

Over the years, I have discovered a variety of methods for attaching or displaying items on flip chart pages. The possibilities are limited only by the imagination. Here are a few ideas to consider.

Suppose you want to add graphics to your flip charts, but do not want to spend hours drawing or tracing them each time you prepare for a class. Consider developing a reusable image library. Begin by (1) copying templates or graphics from this book, (2) finding other images you like from the various software image packages on the market, and/or (3) creating or having someone else create images for you. Cut these out as you would paper dolls, color them to enhance the impact, then attach the images to your flip chart paper by spraying the front of a sheet of paper, or portion of it, with aerosol artist's adhesive. (See Appendix C.) After your presentation, remove and store the graphics. To protect your images and cutouts between presentations, put them in a manila file folder, envelope, or box. Also, to keep them from sticking together while stored, slip a piece of ordinary kitchen wax paper between each image.

If you expect to use certain items for extended periods or in future sessions, it is wise to glue them to a thick piece of paper (cut in the shape of your images), such as lightweight posterboard. You can spray the back of the paper before participants arrive, then hang the images when you are ready to present a topic. The adhesive lasts for a while, so you can remove and rehang the pages several times.

BRIGHT IDEA

For added durability, and to reduce damage from repeated use, you may want to laminate your graphics to avoid having to re-create them later.

If your easel has a metal magnetic backing—or if there is a metallic-backed dry erase board in the room—you can turn it into a display board for graphic cutouts that tie into your presentation theme. Instead of drawing images on a pad, add a bit of variety and movement to your presentation by coloring, then cutting out paper shapes. You can even laminate them for durability. Attach the cutouts to your easel or dry erase the board with small strips of magnetic tape, available at most large office supply stores. (See Appendix C.)

Use Magnetic Strips on Shapes with Metallic Easels

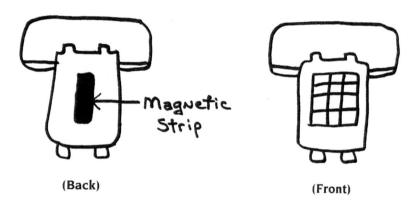

(Back) **(Front)**

Chapter 4

SELECTING THE RIGHT EQUIPMENT AND MATERIALS

THE BASIC TOOL KIT

To help you determine the basic materials and supplies you'll need to conduct a session or meeting. I have listed below the things I typically carry to a training program. You may not always need everything on the list, but my thinking is, "I'd rather have it and not need it, than need it and not have it!"

I suggest you start by assembling a basic "tool box" of items and accessories to carry with you whenever you are going to present. Replenish it after each program religiously and you will likely never get caught without the tools you need to be effective. I have learned too often that relying on others to provide the right supplies or equipment can be an embarrassing and frustrating experience.

To start, invest in a sturdy plastic container or box (preferably with an attached lid) that is large enough to hold at least the items listed below (See the creative presentation resources in Appendix C.):

■ A 12-inch ruler

- Assortment of water-based, colored markers (black, red, dark blue, dark green, brown, yellow, orange, pink)
- Roll of 1-inch (1.75 cm) masking tape
- Small stapler with staples
- Supply of stick or straight pins (stored in a small medicine bottle or film canister)
- Small scissors
- Exacto knife or box cutter (with single-edge blade and protective case)
- Post-it® flip chart tabs
- Pencil
- Art gum eraser (used by graphic artists because it doesn't discolor or tear paper)
- Transparent (invisible) wrapping tape
- Several cloth wall panel clips (see "Unveiling and Displaying Your Masterpieces" in Chapter 7)
- A 9-foot (2.74 m) electrical extension cord with an adapter plug (If training in various countries, carry a plug adapter)
- Several large paper clasps

Depending on the types and number of programs you facilitate, I suggest adding any other items that will help make you successful and enhance the learning of your participants. Following is a discussion of several important items listed above, along with alternatives for them. I also discuss some of the optional equipment you may wish to use: pointers, page protectors, and so on.

TAPE

Masking tape is a staple of any facilitator or trainer. It can be used to tape pages to a wall, hold down loose electrical cords, band markers or other items together, do temporary repairs when something breaks, and perform any number of other useful tasks. Double-sided tape can also be very helpful.

I suggest that you spend a bit more on masking tape to ensure that you obtain a good-quality product, such as Scotch or 3M. My experience is that having tape that holds things well for extended periods of time on a variety of surfaces far outweighs the added money you will spend. There is nothing more frustrating than watching sheets of paper and posters fall off the wall halfway through your presentation. I have also found that the minimum tape width for securely holding paper to a wall for extended periods is 3/4 inch to 1 inch (2.5–5 cm).

An alternative to tape, that I have seen some presenters use, is small pieces of modeling clay. I would caution that some types may damage or leave stains on certain surfaces.

MARKERS

Markers are a tool that every flip charter needs. However, in my experience few presenters think twice about grabbing the first marker they can get their hands on. This is unfortunate, because markers really do differ in quality, design, and function.

For best results when writing on a flip chart, I recommend that you use only water-based markers, which reduce the likelihood of ink "bleeding through" onto the next page. Most permanent and dry erase markers soak through the page and show up on one or more subsequent pages underneath. This is particularly true with less expensive brands of paper, which tend to be thinner and more porous. That is why, as suggested earlier, it is wise to keep a blank page between sheets to protect anything you have prepared on following pages.

A *special note here*: If you are going to hang pages on a wall in a training or conference room for participants to write on, always tape two sheets together to prevent accidental bleed-through. All it takes is one such instance for the hotel or conference manager to dictate, "No taping to the walls." This may not concern you if you don't plan to return to the facility. However, if I am the next presenter there, I will not be happy!

As a rule, do not use permanent ink or dry erase markers on your pages unless you have no other option. The chemicals in dry erase markers are formulated to work best on laminated surfaces (whiteboard). When used on paper, they lose color intensity, and dry out rapidly. Permanent markers are more visible, but they do what they say: They will cause permanent damage to clothing, tablecloths, and wall coverings if you accidentally write on these surfaces. Also, some brands of permanent marker have an overpowering (even nauseating) smell when used extensively. Water-based markers smell better, and some are even flavor-scented (e.g., Mr. Sketch). To ensure that you are getting the right product, read the label. If it says "permanent," keep looking until you find a water-based brand. These are available wherever art, office, and school supplies are sold.

Here is an alternative to water-based markers—for limited use only—that can really add sparkle (literally) to your pages. Visit an art or craft supply store and pick up a few fluorescent, gold, or silver inked markers. Be careful with these and do not get the ink on your clothing, since they are permanent and can stain.

Now for a few tips on using markers:

- Use broad-tipped markers and write with the wider edge to aid visibility of lettering from a distance. If you use fine-tipped markers or turn the widest edge away from the surface, your lines and letters will be extremely narrow. Viewing, especially from a distance, will be extremely difficult.

- Be sure not to leave markers uncapped for long periods of time; they will dry out quickly and add unnecessary expense to your budget. A dry marker can also lead to embarrassment, as you interrupt your presentation to locate a replacement.

- Put your markers down when not using them to write on the flip chart. One of my pet peeves is seeing a facilitator walk around endlessly with a marker, using it as a pointer, capping and uncapping it repeatedly, and generally annoying people by playing with it. Put markers down between uses. It is easy, without thinking about it, to fall into a pattern of playing with markers as you speak. This can undermine an otherwise perfect presentation.

POINTERS

If you like to use pointers to focus attention on key words or concepts that you have flip-charted, you have a variety of options. They run from the mundane to the creative. Here are some "pointers" on common and not so common pointers:

Wooden Dowel Rods
Most audiovisual and art supply stores carry traditional wooden pointers. They are typically about 3 feet (914 m) long with a black

rubber or painted tip. If you cannot find one, go to a craft, home supply, or hardware store and ask for a wooden dowel rod, the kind used to support thin curtains. To create the black tip, simply touch up the end with flat black paint.

Dowel Rod **Collapsible Metal Pointer** **Lighted Infrared Pointer**

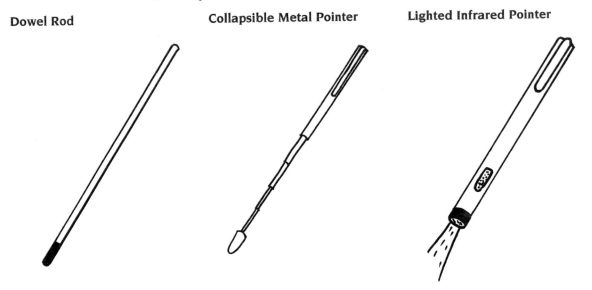

Collapsible Metal Pointers
Similar to the antennas on some cars, collapsible pointers are favored by many presenters. Some even have a clip, similar to an ink pen, so they can be carried in the pocket.

Lighted Infrared Pointers
Battery-operated infrared pointers are the latest fad. They project a small red beam of light, thereby allowing you to stand across the room and "point" by projecting the red dot on your flip chart page. A downside is that even experienced presenters have difficulty holding the light steady. This gives the nonverbal appearance of nervousness and can be distracting as the dot dances around the page. A more serious concern is that the laser light can cause eye damage if you accidentally look into it or project it into the eyes of an attendee.

Pointers with Pizzazz
If you really want to add some pizzazz and break the monotony, here are two creative ideas:

- Draw a 3-foot (.914 m) *directional shape* (e.g., a long arm with a finger pointing, an arrow, a long ink pen or pencil, a long-nosed animal) on cardboard or posterboard. Brightly color the shape, then cut it out. You can laminate it to add strength and protect it. (See the templates in Part IV Appendix A for sample images to copy).

Sample Cardboard Shapes

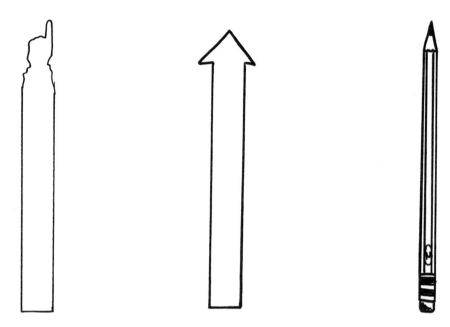

- Purchase a *long pencil* and use it as a pointer. Pencil pointers run to several feet in length. (See the Think BIG! listing in Appendix C.)

Plucked Chicken Pointer

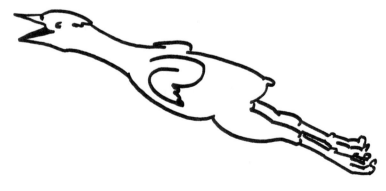

- Use a hard rubber chicken—that's right, I said chicken! These humorous props can add levity to any presentation or simply show that you are not "chicken" when it comes to making your point clear. (See the Creative Presentation Resources entry in Appendix C.)

Here are four key tips on using pointers:

1. When you are through pointing at your flip chart, put the pointer down! It is too tempting to play with it or point at other things, such as participants. Either habit can be distracting, and you might even accidentally throw the pointer toward a participant.

2. Hold the pointer in the hand closest to the flip chart for ease of access to the pad.

3. If you are using a collapsible pointer, do not play with it by extending and retracting as you talk. Remember not to point it toward a person.

4. If using a laser pointer, NEVER project toward a participant.

PAPER

Standard Paper Pads

There are a variety of paper pads on the market. The optimal size is 27" × 34" (.6 m × .86 m), which fits correctly on most standard easels. I encourage you to spend the extra money and get the heavier-quality paper. Some of the less expensive types are akin to the porous writing tablets used by children in elementary school. This paper is harder to work with and often extremely difficult to tear from a pad. Also, it may allow ink to bleed through onto subsequent pages. Stick with heavier plain or lined paper in yellow or white. There is even one type with light blue grid lines. All three types work well for those of us who have difficulty writing in a straight line, or who need to make technical presentations with graphs.

Alternative Paper

Many years ago, I had to create a running series of images for a program I was conducting over a period of months. Initially, I tried taping pages together side by side. After I put the pages up and took them down several times, I realized this was not the best idea. They kept falling apart as the glue on the tape failed, and after a while I had to re-create all eight or nine pages. Then I hit upon an idea while I was at my local meat market. I noticed the butcher tearing white paper from a large roll. Aha! I saw an alternative to pad paper—and the rest, as they say, is history. Butcher paper worked beautifully.

So, if you want to use long sheets of paper to line a wall for a special activity or presentation, you should consider going to a grocery supply store to purchase a roll of plain white butcher paper (not the waxed kind). You can cut the paper to any length desired, so you can create individual sheets for participants to write or draw on for activities. This is a more work-intensive way to get standard-size paper; however, it also saves precious budget dollars. You can even create makeshift pads for your easel. Do this by cutting sheets at the standard pad size (27" × 34"), punch holes at the top edges, and attach the pages together with a clip, staple, or other device.

Self-Adhesive Pads

Another update to the standard newsprint flip chart has appeared on the market. This new pad has adhesive along the top edge of each page (similar to the Post-it notes with which you are probably familiar) and is standard flip chart size. Sheets torn off the pad can be affixed to most wall surfaces without tape, causing no damage to walls. And the pages can be removed easily and relocated.

A variation of the self-adhesive pads is a roll of paper that comes in a roller-type container with a handle. You can pull out any length needed up to 75 feet (22.85 m). The paper has adhesive along the top and bottom back edges so you can literally paper the wall and have a writing surface around the room. The containers can be hand-held or hung from an easel.

Portable Roll of Self-Adhesive Paper

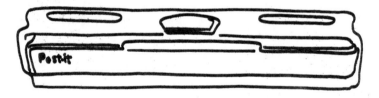

BRIGHT IDEA

An alternative to the large Post-it pads is create your own self-adhesive paper. You can do this by purchasing roll-on containers of glue or artist's spray adhesive to put on the back of your sheets. *Note*: Always test the brand of glue you have purchased on an obscure area of the wall to ensure that no damage results—some fabric wall surfaces might discolor. Also, the spray usually has a strong odor. Always follow the instructions on the package and use it in a ventilated area. Keep in mind that some participants may have allergies or respiratory conditions, so use the spray *before* they arrive.

Vinyl Dry Erase Pads

Another really interesting, and helpful, product to hit the market in recent years is the vinyl dry erase pad. These individual sheets adhere to most wall surfaces by static electricity. Simply write on them, tear off, and slap them up on the wall. They are removable as well as erasable when used with dry erase markers (the kind used on "whiteboard"). Two brand names for these products are Static Images™ by 3M and Wall Write™ by Permacharge. (See Appendix C.)

PAGE PROTECTORS

Just as you protect your 81/2" × 11" (21.5 cm × 28 cm) pages by enclosing them in plastic document protectors, so you can safeguard your flip chart pages. Several companies have developed polypropylene (plastic) protectors that accommodate sheets up to 27" × 34" (.6 m × .86 m). You can predraw your title lines and graphics on paper, then slip each page into a protector. You can then capture participants' comments by writing on the plastic protectors with wet or dry erase markers. When the session is over, wipe the pages off as you would a dry erase board, store them, and you are ready for the next program. Page protectors significantly reduce wear and tear in storage and transport, but do add significantly to weight. Keep this in mind if you are using storage techniques that involve hanging the pads from the wall on pegs.

Flip Chart Poster Frame

If you do use protectors, you will also need extenders to hang the assembled page on the easel. These are simple pieces of flat steel, with a washer, screw, and wing nut. You may have to get the steel pieces drilled to fit the screw and easel pad pegs. An easier way is to buy them ready-made from an audiovisual supply store. (See the Trainer's Warehouse listing in Appendix C.)

An additional option on the market is a semirigid plastic envelope, into which you can slide flip chart pages. Like the plastic protectors, they are the standard 27" × 34". These innovative items give the appearance that your pages are in a frame. If you are creating posters with graphics or quoted text, as described earlier, you can frame them in these devices for a really polished, professional look. (See the Trainer's Warehouse entry in Appendix C.)

Flip Chart Easel Extenders

Flip Chart Poster Frame

FLIP CHART
POSTER FRAME

TACKS AND PINS

Stick pins, thumb tacks, and/or straight pins come in handy as a backup for tape, especially in an environment that has corkboard strips around the room. In environments that have draperies covering a large portion of the wall, but little usable wall surface, the straight pins (the kind used by tailors or seamstresses) can be used to attach pages of paper to curtain material without causing damage.

EASELS: FOLDING AND ADJUSTABLE MODELS

Flip chart easel designs have changed over the past decade and they continue to do so. A solid metal construction is no longer your only choice. Today you can get easels in double widths, with magnetic, dry erase, and chalkboard backing, legs that fold, retract, extend, or detach, and many other optional features. "You get what you pay for" definitely applies to flip charts and associated materials. As always, some tools are more useful and appropriate than others. Let's look at several of the folding and adjustable models.

Portable Frame with Retractable Legs

Portable frames come in two designs. One has legs locked in place with a tightening nut that puts tension on the upper leg and holds the lower leg in place. The second has small spring-loaded pins that project through holes in the upper leg tube and hold the lower leg in place.

Pros. Usually of an A-frame aluminum construction, portable models are very lightweight and convenient. I have found them to be useful for displaying flip chart pads on which I will not be writing, as well as posters or signs. Some models have a small crossbar that connects and holds the legs in position. Another nice feature about the tripod units is that they are easy to transport and require little storage space. Many come with carrying cases for transporting.

Cons. Because portable frames are so lightweight, their legs can become bent and nonretractable. Also, as mentioned earlier, the models that have legs locked in place with removable screws can create problems if the screws fall off and get lost. These frames also require a bit of juggling to hold the leg in position as you adjust the screw. Some people have difficulty manipulating the legs.

The models with tightening nuts are easier to work with; however, the nuts can become stripped out and make locking in place impossible. When this happens, the easel can slowly sink under weight of paper. Because of their lightweight construction, these models make writing on a page shaky and a bit tedious. As mentioned earlier, two hands are needed to manipulate the nut and pull at the leg extension. Another drawback is that many models have no place for holding markers.

Paper is held in place in one of two ways. Some models have a short bar with two rubber nubs that rest against the top crossbar. To put paper in, you move the bar up slightly, insert the pad, then pull the bar back down. The rubber nubs put pressure on the pad and hold it in place. Since this bar is mobile and the frame is unsteady, writing can be a real challenge. Other models have a clamp-type bar across the top for holding paper. Putting pressure on the bar opens enough space under it for pad insertion. Once the pad is in place, the bar is released. If the spring clamp becomes weak, the pad can slip.

Frames with Retractable Legs

While on the subject of the A-frame easel, let me suggest a relatively new product attachment to add a bit of stability to this stand. It is a folding backboard panel that has two riveted holes at the top. It folds accordion style and, along with the A-frame easel, fits into a vinyl carrying case. Once you attach the backboard, you can use either the vinyl dry erase surface pages or a regular flip chart pad to write on. I have not yet used one of these devices. It seems that, beyond gaining a bit of support for writing on the wobbly stand—which is innovative enough—you gain little else of value. (See the Trainer's Warehouse listing in Appendix C.)

Folding Backboard Panel

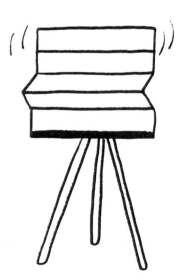

Solid-Backed Metal Easel with Folding Legs

Pros. The older, solid-backed metal easels are still around and I occasionally run into them in organizations. Thanks to their heavy construction, they provide a relatively stable writing surface. Construction is relatively simple. Because the paper pad is held in place with a clip-type bar at the front, top portion of the easel, the paper can be changed by one person. Most also have a tray (sometimes removable) to hold markers. For added versatility, some models can be used for tabletop displays, when their legs are folded. Other brands have brackets on the back to hold markers during storage.

Cons. As with anything else, a strength carried to an extreme becomes a weakness. Because of their solid construction, these metal easels weigh quite a bit. This makes moving and transport awkward, especially for smaller-framed facilitators. Disabled presenters may also have difficulty moving the easel or changing the paper by themselves. Finally, because the folding legs are movable, the locking mechanism sometimes wears out. The legs can pinch your fingers if you are not careful.

Solid-Backed Metallic Easel with Folding Legs

Solid-Backed, Magnetic, Fiberglass Whiteboard Easel with Folding Legs

Pros. Unlike the heavier models, the fiberglass whiteboard easels are highly portable at around 20 pounds. Some manufacturers even provide a weatherproof nylon carrying case. Like its solid metal relative, this model provides a relatively stable writing surface as a standing or tabletop surface. In addition to allowing you to hang a pad of paper, it provides the option of a magnetic, dry erase writing surface. With that feature, you can attach tent-sized placards with text instead of using flip chart paper. And, since the cards are reusable—especially if you laminate them—they are more durable and easier to store.

Downward pressure holds the paper in place against the backboard with a clip-type bar at the top front. Again, the paper can be changed by one person, since it simply slides up under the clip. Typically, this model has a tray to hold markers.

Because the legs often form a complete U shape and are held in the extended position by large plastic locking knobs on either side, more stability is gained over models with four independent legs. For added versatility, the writing surface can be locked at a horizontal level to hold supplies or other equipment. Also, the writing surface can be lowered and locked in place between the legs. The result is a reduced-height table easel for business presentations.

One manufacturer offers a pressure-type bar under an overhanging extension at the top of the easel to hold paper in place. To insert it, you simply push the top of the pad up and under the bar. Once released, the bar is held in place by downward pressure, making it very easy to put a pad onto the easel.

Cons. Because of their many features, some models may have a prohibitive cost. However, as with anything else, there are bargains. I recently saw one marked down from $149 to $99 in an office supply store.

As with many models, a person with limited use of the hands or arms may have trouble changing paper unless the easel is lying flat on the floor or is locked in the horizontal position. The magnetic whiteboard provides a viable alternative to the pads, but limits some versatility in moving information around on paper. An additional drawback is that the locking knob may break, making it impossible to secure the legs into position.

Since dry erase boards and flip chart paper require different types of markers, care is needed not to use the wrong marker when writing. Additionally, the spring-loaded bar, mentioned above, can become a negative if the spring weakens. With lesser the tension, the pad can slip out.

Solid-Backed Magnetic, Fiberglass Whiteboard Easel with Folding Legs

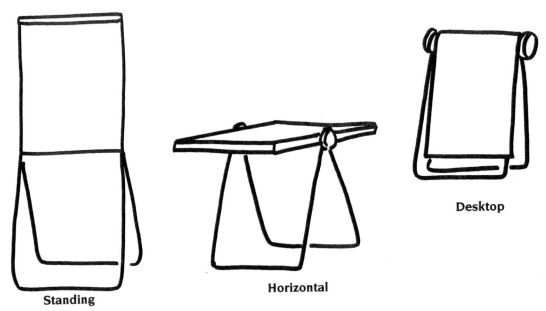

Desktop

Horizontal

Standing

BRIGHT IDEA
There are commercial products available for removing permanent and water-based ink marks from whiteboard surfaces when mistakes are made or the wrong type of marker is used. Windex or similar solutions also work relatively well. As a quick fix, if you inadvertently write with a permanent marker, rewrite over the letters with the same marker. While the ink is still wet, immediately wipe it off with a paper towel. This removes the bulk of the ink. Even though a slight shadow may remain, you can continue your presentation. Later, you can remove remnants of the marks with commercial solutions.

Adjustable-Height Easel

Pros. As with the previous model, the adjustable easel can be used for flip chart pads, or as a dry erase or magnetic display surface. Some models have a chalkboard surface instead of the dry erase surface.

Adjustable Height Easel

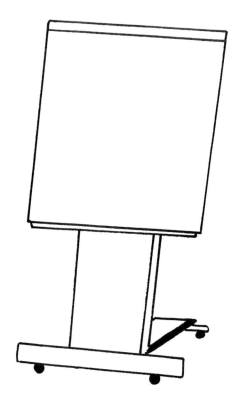

One thing I like about this model is that the writing area can be adjusted from 74 inches to 91 inches (1.8–2.6 m) to suit the a facilitator's height. In addition, some models have extension arms that can be opened on either side of the back to allow display of additional pads (although there is no backing for writing on these pads). To move the easel from one point to another, you simply roll them because they have caster-type wheels. Once in position, the front caster has a foot-locking mechanism to keep it stationary until you are ready for additional movement.

All this, and it comes with a mounted marker tray!

Cons. As with the other models, there are some negatives. For example, the adjustable-height easel costs more than a standard easel without all the bells and whistles. And because it is more bulky, it is not as portable for moving to other training sites. Finally, because these models are adjustable and have a higher profile, storage may be more of a challenge.

Lightweight Fiberglass Whiteboard Easel

Pros. If you are looking for a simpler piece of equipment, fiberglass whiteboard may be to your liking. This is a good basic easel. Because these models are lighter than the previous models discussed, moving and handling are easier.

In addition, they are less expensive than their heavier counterparts, so you can use your training dollars for other supplies and materials. As with previous models, you have the option of either writing on the dry erase white surface or using a flip chart pad. Some models have a removable bar across the top to hold the paper pad in place.

Cons. Since the lightweight model is simpler, it also leaves some things to be desired. For example, many models do not have marker trays. However, don't let that deter you. Remember my earlier tip for makeshift trays.

**Lightweight Fiberglass
Whiteboard Easel**

One feature that creates a challenge is that these easels are not as sturdy as the heavier models; therefore, they can be a bit unstable as a writing surface. Some have collapsible legs held in place by locking nuts that sometimes malfunction, causing the legs to retract slowly while the easel is in use. (You'll read about an embarrassing incident I had, later in Chapter 7. This is the easel I was using!)

One more frustrating feature (or lack of one), in my opinion, is that some models have no retaining device for pads. They simply have two pegs at the top where the paper pad is hung.

Two final areas of concern is that the bar holding the paper pad in place on some models is attached with two removable screws. These can get lost. Also, you need two hands to manipulate the bar, screws, and paper and may have trouble by yourself. Some facilitators solve the problem by attaching a pad first by laying the easel on a flat surface.

BRIGHT IDEA
To secure paper on this type of easel if only pegs exist, I often use one of those super-size rubber bands available at office supply stores. After putting my pad on the easel, I stretch the band between the pegs to secure the paper. String works well too, but takes more time to put on and take off.

EASELS: ONE-PIECE SOLID CONSTRUCTION

Solid-Backed Metal Easel with Removable Crossbar

The solid-backed metal easel, one of the older designs, is still readily available and in use by many trainers and presenters.

Pros. This was one of the first types of easels I used as a presenter in the 1970s. It is made of heavy-gauge steel, so it provides a relatively stable writing surface that can also be used to attach images with magnetic backings. It also typically has a tray for holding markers. As discussed before, some models also have folding legs for easier storage.

**Solid-Backed, Metal Easel
with Removable Crossbar**

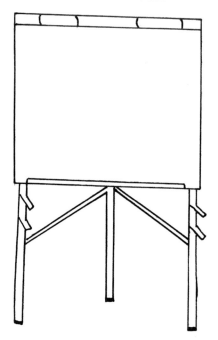

Cons. The worst feature on these models, in my opinion, is that the pad retaining bar is removable. It is held in place by two long screws that go through the bar, pad, and frame, then are locked in place by a wing nut on the back. I rarely ever find one that has the nuts still in place (at least not the originals). This is because they often come loose, fall off, or get lost and need to be replaced at the hardware store. Another downside of the removable bar is that it often takes two people, or at least some degree of dexterity, to change the pad of paper while the flip chart is standing.

The weight and design of solid-backed easels pose a challenge when transporting and storing them, especially older models that do not even have folding legs. To compound their inefficiency, some models do not offer marker trays as standard equipment.

BRIGHT IDEA

Here's an emergency solution for securing your paper pad on an easel that has a solid bar held on its frame by two screws but is missing the wing nuts or clips. Try stretching a large, thick rubber band from one screw to the other on the back of the easel. This creates tension and pull the screw stems together, holding the paper in place. String works as an alternative.

Lightweight Sliding Molded Plastic Easel

Although molded plastic is a relative newcomer to the easel market, several distributors have this model. Features and design are similar among manufacturers.

Pros. Because these easels are made of a relatively lightweight, high-impact plastic material, transportation is easier. Some models are spring-loaded and work by sliding the entire upper portion of the frame down over the leg portion for compact, easy storage. Still other models have a white laminated backing or a magnetic dry erase writing surface, thereby increasing presentation options. Marker trays are standard and paper is held in place by a pressure bar.

**Lightweight Sliding
Molded Plastic Easel**

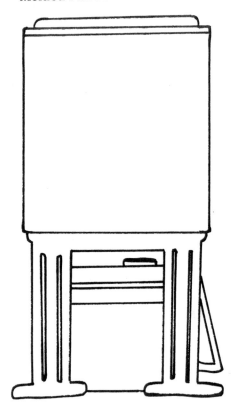

Cons. To pay for the convenience and versatility, some manufacturers have attached a higher price tag to these models compared with some of the other models discussed. As with any moving parts, spring mechanisms sometimes malfunction after excessive use. When this occurs, the chart may slowly sink under the weight of the paper pad during your presentation. And, as with other models, people with limited use of their hands or arms could face a challenge setting up the easel on their own. To raise the upper portion of the easel, you must stand behind it, put your feet on the two "feet" (one on either side), grasp the top portion, and pull up. Because the unit is made of plastic, there is a bit of resistance as the plastic top pulls against the plastic bottom.

Another potential problem is that the plastic "lip" that extends in front of the cutout areas to prevent the markers from rolling off the shelves is very low. This allows markers to fall often. A final concern is that the two pins at the top of the easel, under the pad tension bar, are very short. This limits you to placing only one pad on the easel at a time.

BRIGHT IDEA

I recently read about two products that can help in transporting and moving your flip chart easels. The first is a two-wheel carriage that is tall enough to carry a collapsible easel. The easel is held in place by elastic bungee cords during transport. These are modified versions of the small carts used to transport luggage. The second item is a metal wheel adapter that fits onto the round or rectangular legs of most flip chart easels. Once you slip these around the base of the easel legs, you Velcro them into place, then simply roll your flip chart around the room instead of dragging or carrying it. Although this feature may not seem like a big deal, I can see its value for many facilitators. (See the Trainer's Warehouse listing in Appendix C.)

BUILD YOUR OWN EASEL

What do you do when you are going to a facility that either does not have flip chart easels or charges exorbitant fees to rent them? The answer—create your own! There is certainly no shortage of choices for commercially produced flip chart easels, but in some situations you may not have access to one of the fancy ones. Or there may be instances when you simply prefer a solid, yet inexpensive alternative.

I can think of a couple of times in one of my past lives when I could have benefited from a sturdy makeshift easel on the spot. For example, in the Marine Corps I often found myself in an outdoors environment giving short presentations or briefings. Often these occurred under a picnic-style canopy, but more likely they were in a tent or under a tree. A flip chart easel would have sharpened my presentations.

Likewise, when I was a Cub Scout leader for a group of local boys and wanted to give an instant class on first aid in the woods, an easel and pad would have helped hold their attention and paint a better picture for them.

In either case, I know that I would not have wanted to take a $300 flip chart easel out into the elements of nature. That is where my improvised models come in handy. These work really well whenever you have to give presentations to a group outdoors, such as on a construction site or at an outdoor management retreat. They are heavier and can be leaned against a wall or tree or raised up on a chair for better visibility. Here are two different ways to build one of your own.

Makeshift Easel 1

You will need the following materials and tools to get started:

- Electric drill and drill bits
- Two 2 1/4-inch (5.25 cm) screws with washers and wing nuts to match
- A piece of plywood about 30" × 40" (.76 m × 1.02 m)
- A strip of wood the size of a yard or meter stick
- Two large cans of black, flat spray paint (optional)
- An elastic bungee cord or rope (long enough to go around the width of the plywood and a chair back)

Tools and Supplies for Building Your Own Easel
From Left to Right: **Electric Drill, Black Spray Paint, Screws**
Middle: **Plywood and Wooden Strip**
Bottom: **Bungee Cord/Rope**

To get started, go to a lumberyard (or a neighbor's back yard) and get the size of plywood you need. Next visit a hardware store to buy two screws long enough to fit through the wood strip, paper pad, and backboard with a little to spare, and metal washers and wing nuts to hold the device together. If you'd like to make your end product a bit more aesthetically pleasing, buy two cans of black spray paint while you are there. Also pick up a couple of bungee cords or lengths of cotton rope (for use in strapping the easel back to a chair or table when you use it).

Okay, you are now ready! Lay the board on a flat surface with the narrower edge facing the top. Make sure you select a spot where you can safely drill holes for the screws. Next, position your paper pad so that the top edge, with the holes, is at the top edge of the plywood. Center the pad on the wood and mark through the holes. Do the same with the wooden strip by placing it under the pad and marking the hole locations.

You are now ready to drill the two pieces. Choose a drill bit slightly larger than your screw width (5/16 inch, or 80 mm) and carefully drill holes in the locations marked earlier. After you have your holes completed, you can spray-paint the wooden surfaces if desired. You will likely need several coats of paint, since plywood is very porous and absorbs it. When the board is ready to use, place the pad on top of the plywood, then put the wooden strip on top. Line up the holes for all three; insert the screws through the washers, then through the strip, pad, and backboard; attach the wing nuts to the back to secure all the pieces in place.

For legs, place the easel on a metal-framed, straight-backed conference room chair. You are now ready to present! The plywood is rather heavy and a bit awkward to balance, so use a piece of rope or elastic bungee cord to wrap around the easel back and chair to hold it in place. You can add height for better participant viewing by placing the chair on a tabletop. I find that it is easier to put the chair in place before adding the easel.

Another option for legs is to use one of the heavy-duty poster stands found in many hotel or conference facilities.

Improvised Easel on Chair   **Improvised Easel on Posterstand**

Makeshift Easel 2

A second makeshift easel can be found in virtually any conference or training room in the form of a 4' × 6' (1.3 m × 1.9 m) folding table. By flipping the table on end, you can create an emergency easel. The only materials you will need are two large metal "bull clips" from an office supply store, or similar clamping devices from a hardware store, to hold the pad in place. An alternative is simply to use the table as a backing to tape paper onto. The key is to ensure that the table is balanced and stable to prevent it from falling over or causing injury.

Impromptu Easel

Chapter 5

Flip Chart Logistics: Overcoming the "Hassle Factor"

OPTIONS FOR HANGING FLIP CHARTS ON WALLS—SO THEY STAY HUNG

There are many ways to display your flip chart pages once they are created. Depending on the room and equipment available, you may be able to use one or more of the following techniques.

Masking Tape

One of the quickest and easiest ways to hang a page is by using a roll of 1-inch (2.5 cm) wide masking tape. Simply tear two strips off the roll and apply one to each of the top corners of the page. Next rip the page from the pad and post it on the wall. *Note:* Be sure to get permission, since some facilities frown upon using tape for fear of damage to the wall finish or paint surface. This concern is basically unfounded if you are using fresh, top-quality (3M, Scotch, or other name brand) tape.

BRIGHT IDEA

Attach 2-inch to 4-inch (5–10 cm) strips of masking tape along the side of your easel or leg of your tripod before your presentation. This allows you quick access to tape when you finish a page and want to tape it to the wall for further reference.

Make Tape Available on the Edge of Your Easel

Another way of applying tape, which I use primarily for attaching pages or posters to the wall before my participants arrive, is to form strips of masking tape approximately 2 to 3 inches (5–7.5 cm) long into a small circle. Loop the ends until they stick together with the glue side out. Put several of these circles on the back side of the page, at the top and bottom, then attach the page to the wall.

BRIGHT IDEA

To reduce wear and damage to predrawn flip chart pages that you regularly tape to a wall, try permanently affixing a 3" × 2" (7.5 × 5 cm) strip of masking tape on the back of each page at each corner. You can then attach the rolled pieces of tape, as discussed above, on top of the strips whenever you need to use the page. This decreases the chance of ripping your paper, since you are pulling tape from tape as opposed to tape from paper.

Reduce Wear on Pages with Permanently Affixed Tape on Reverse

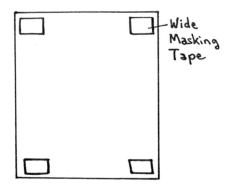

Double-Sided Masking Tape

Some time ago, a friend of mine introduced me to a really helpful product. And, although it is sometimes difficult to find, it provides a handy alternative to putting tape on each page you hang. The product is double-sided tape (sticky surface on both sides). When I can get it, especially if I'm doing a full day or multiday program, I hang a strip along the length of the wall at a height of 6" to 7"(1.8–2.1 m). I can then quickly tape and remove pages as necessary throughout the program and I do not have to fumble with a roll of masking tape.

BRIGHT IDEA

If you are having participants draw or write ideas on a flip chart page during an activity, you can make masking tape easily accessible by wrapping a small amount around a marker then giving it to each participant. When needed, all the user has to do is unwrap and tape. This saves having to pass around rolls or having to tear pieces of tape for distribution.

Masking Tape Wrapped around a Marker

Multipurpose Labels

An alternative to masking tape for attaching your pages to a wall is to use the small, round adhesive labels (minimum 1-1/4 inch works best) that are often used to seal catalogs or to label files in an office. Two or three of these stuck to the top right and left corner of the paper are fine substitutes, and in some cases may be preferable to masking tape. These typically come in packages of 500 or more, and can be obtained at most office supply or packing/shipping stores.

Use Multipurpose Labels to Hang Pages

Cloth Panel Wall Clips

I have recently discovered that, with the proliferation of cloth-covered modular cubicles in today's offices, a really practical solution to hanging papers on walls has been invented. These are small plastic clasp devices that have two little pins on the back. The pins can slip into the cloth without damaging the material and can hold up to 40 sheets of paper. They are perfect for cloth-covered hotel, conference room, and training room walls when no tape is allowed.

Cloth Panel Wall Clips

Stick Pins or Thumb Tacks

Here's a more permanent solution to hanging items in conference and training rooms or attaching paper around the perimeter of any room. Simply hang a narrow wooden strip with corkboard (similar to that found on bulletin boards) at a height of approximately 7 feet (2.1 m). You can then use bulletin board stick pins or thumb tacks to attach your pages. These strips are usually available in office, art, hobby, and school supply stores where presentation materials are sold.

Hang Paper with Stick Pins

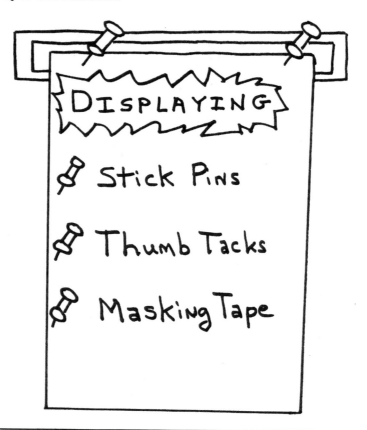

Metal Strips

Another, more permanent strategy is to mount 2-inch (5 cm) metal strips around the walls. Ensure that you use a metal to which magnets will attach (i.e., not aluminum). You can then use standard refrigerator or note magnets in different shapes to hold paper. Magnetic-backed paper clamps, available at many home or office supply stores, are generally better for holding single sheets rather than pads of paper. (See the Creative Presentation Resources entry in Appendix C.) As I mentioned earlier, these clamps are also good for attaching items to metal easels and dry erase boards.

As an alternative, you can purchase rolls of magnetic tape at office supply stores or through office supply catalogs. (See Appendix C.) Cut off small strips to hold pages to the metal.

Wooden Strips

As with metal strips, you can mount wooden ones to the walls (painted to blend with wall color). Put large nails at various intervals to correspond to flip chart paper width, which is 27 inches (.68 m). Place the nails at approximately 2 and 25 inches (5.08 and 63 cm) rather than at the very ends of the paper width. Next, either nail standard wooden, spring-type clothespins or hang the heavy-duty metal "bull clips" along the strip. You can then hang flip chart pages, as needed.

Mounted Wooden Strips with Metal Clips

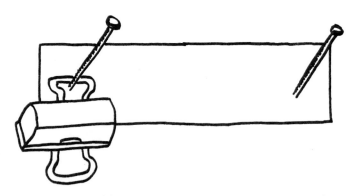

Cloth Panel Adhesive Strips

Another device relatively new to the market and designed for use in the modular office environment is an adhesive-backed tab that is similar to Velcro on one side. These tabs can be attached to the backs of pages and then hung on any cloth-covered conference or training room wall. In addition, if you have laminated your images, or have developed strips of text and mounted them on strips of posterboard, you can now attach these tabs to the reverse side of your artwork and hang them directly on a cloth wall without using flip chart paper. Imagine the versatility of being able to move words, images, and phrases around in any order as you speak. This is a modern-day version of the cloth board technique we will look at next. You can find these strips in office supply stores.

Cloth Boards

Although not directly related to use with flip chart paper, here's an idea that has been around for decades and can still be used in conjunction with a flip chart easel. Creative teachers, instructors, and presenters have used cloth board (sometimes called felt or flannel boards) in a variety of ways for years. They can add a new dimension to the static presentation of information without the need for flip chart paper.

Attaching Cloth to Cardboard or Plywood

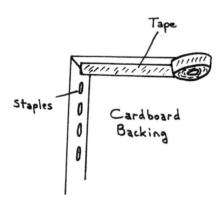

To make one, take a piece of dark flannel or felt, or some rough-weave material such as cotton terrycloth. This will serve as a display surface. Next, drape the material over an easel and secure it to the back with tape, clothespins, or clamps. To create a reusable board, start with a piece of cardboard or plywood that is at least the size of a flip chart pad. Drape it with your material, then staple, tape, or glue the edges along the back of the cardboard or plywood.

To accompany this helpful tool, create *flash cards* and attach small strips of Velcro (or the cloth adhesive strips discussed earlier) to the back of them. You can then build your message for participants one line at a time. Follow these steps:

- Cut strips of posterboard to the desired card size.
- Write your text on them—a separate title card and one thought, topic, sentence, or idea per card.
- Cut 1-inch (2.5 cm) pieces of the barbed (adhesive) portion of your Velcro strip.
- Glue or tape the Velcro to the backs of your flash cards.

Velcro Strips for Flash Cards

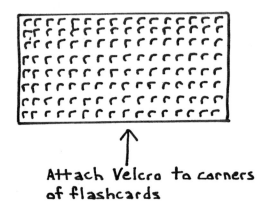

Attach Velcro to corners of flashcards

You're now ready to present! As you discuss your topics, simply attach the pasteboard strips to the material. You can also hang the cloth material from a wall to provide an additional presentation surface and save your easel for other uses. An alternative is to apply your cards directly to the cloth-covered wall in a hotel or training room by simply pushing them against the rough cloth surface. The barbs cling and your cards stay put.

TRANSPORTING FLIP CHARTS SAFELY

If you are like me, once you spend hours agonizing over what to put on your predrawn flip charts and then painstakingly sketch and draw your ideas, you want to get as much use from them as possible. This may be difficult if you take your training on the road.

To ship a flip chart pad safely, consider one of the following options.

Laminating Pages

To preserve individual flip chart pages, you can purchase a lamination machine that can handle flip chart or poster-size pages. Some can even laminate computer-generated banners. If you would rather not buy your own equipment, there are companies that can provide this service for you. (See Appendix C.) You can also hang blank laminated pages on an easel to create an erasable writing surface.

Cardboard Mailing Tubes

Cardboard tubes are available through many sources, including the U.S. Postal Service. (See Appendix C.) Because of the curling that occurs when the charts are rolled and then taken out for use, tubes are not the preferred method of storage and shipment. However, they do provide a means of protecting your flip charts from damage. For maximum protection, the tubes should be the larger variety, approximately 4-1/4 inches (11.5 cm) in diameter, in order to lessen the curling effect. Before rolling and inserting the pads, cut all but 2 or 3 inches (5–7.5 cm) of the cardboard attached to the rear of the pad. This reduces the amount of curl once you unroll the pad.

If your tube is longer than your rolled pad, wad it with paper, cloth, bubble wrap packing material, or the small Styrofoam "popcorn" packing pieces used in shipping products. This fills the empty space and helps prevent the pad from banging up and down against the end of the tube. Roll your charts from the bottom with the printed side facing out so they will curl less on the easel once you remove them from the carrying case. Putting a rubber band or string around them helps keep the charts stationary and rolled tightly.

A technique I use for quickly locating stored flip charts is to write the name of the program in bold letters on the outside of the tube.

Cardboard Mailing Tube with Program Name

BRIGHT IDEA

Here's a technique I picked up from author and presenter Richard Brandt to protect wooden pointers, yardsticks, or meter sticks during transport. Brandt always inserted the items into the center of his rolled flip chart pad in a shipping or storage tube. This eliminates having to carry them separately and provides protection against breakage.

Plastic Carrying Case

Plastic Carrying Tubes

A variation on the cardboard mailing tubes are hard plastic tubes with detachable shoulder straps. There is even a version that can be extended in length. These are excellent for the traveling trainer.

BRIGHT IDEA

If you do not have a shipping tube but need to transport a pad post haste to a training site, try this. Cut off the hard cardboard backing, leaving a 2-inch (5 cm) strip along the top, bound edge. You can easily roll up the pad and secure it with rubber bands at either end.

Make sure you have a blank page in front of your program cover sheet. This provides protection for the first page your participants will see. Remember, first impressions are lasting ones.

Cardboard Panels

Here's another technique for transporting and storing your charts. Cut two sections of cardboard pieces slightly larger than the size of your flip chart pad. Place pads between the two pieces, then tape or staple the cardboard pieces together with heavy-duty staples. Cover all four edges of the cardboard with plastic shipping tape to form a protective container. You can achieve the same results by simply retaining the original box that the pad came in when you purchased it. The box is the perfect size and can be retaped to hold your pad in place and protect it.

Artist's Portfolio with Pad

Artist's Portfolio

For a snappy alternative, try a leather artist's portfolio with carrying handles and zippers, available at art or office supply stores. There are less expensive and less durable cardboard versions that you can get for short trips across town. I do not recommend the latter for airline travel, especially since you will have to check it as luggage.

Easel Transport

If you have no other option, or simply desire to transport your pads on an easel, you can still provide some degree of protection by tying a piece of rope or bungee cord around the bottom of the pad and easel. This can help prevent damage by the wind or external objects. Turning the pad over so that the cardboard backing faces out provides additional protection.

Transporting Pad on an Easel

CREATING REUSABLE FLIP CHARTS

Hanging Laminated Pages

If you have ever wanted to create reusable flip chart pages, you can. Laminate your flip chart pages, put holes at the top to correspond with your easel, then go to a school supply or variety store to buy looseleaf binder rings. Metal shower curtain rings, available at any hardware store, will work as well.

Arrange the pages you want on the rings, then insert a 1/2-inch wooden dowel (1.25 cm) through both rings. Next take two or three sections of coat hanger or heavy wire, each 6 to 8 inches (16–22 cm) long, and form them into an S shape. Hang each over the top of a solid-backed easel, and then hang your dowel rod across them. Depending on the number of pages you are using, you may have to find other material or metal wire stronger than a hanger to support the weight.

This technique adds flexibility to your presentations without the need to copy or re-create posters already developed.

IMPROVING YOUR EASEL

If you are a recovering perfectionist like me, even though you occasionally miss a meeting of Perfectionists Anonymous, you will most likely hate the fact that many manufacturers just do not design their flip chart easels to fit your needs. Specifically, there is never enough room for markers on the easel. I often find myself laying markers on a chair or table, where they are too far away when I need them or simply roll onto the floor. I have developed two ways of dealing with manufacturers' ineptitude.

Create a Marker Tray

If you have ever had to use an easel that has no marker tray, then this idea is for you. To create a tray for markers, cut a strip 3 to 4 inches (7.5–10 cm) from the bottom edge of the cardboard backing on a flip chart paper pad. Form it into an L shape and then tape it along the bottom and at the corners of the flip chart where the marker tray would normally be. Instant tray!

Creating Your Own Marker Tray

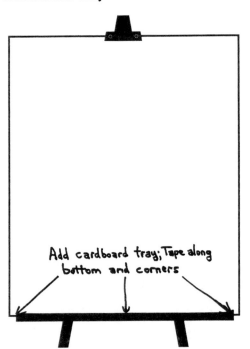

Add cardboard tray; Tape along bottom and corners

Wire Mesh Marker Tray

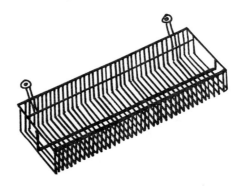

Add a "Caddy"

Assuming the flip chart easel belongs to you or your company, try this related idea. (If you are renting the easel or using someone else's, I suggest getting permission first.) Visit a local home products store that sells wire mesh shelving (also see Appendix C) and ask for an "all-purpose caddy." Drill two holes in the bottom of your flip chart easel. Next, attach the caddy through the drilled holes with a couple of metal screws. The caddy holds several markers as well as tape and other stuff and virtually eliminates having to pick markers up from the floor.

An alternate technique, for easels that already have marker trays, is to clamp the caddy to the front edge of the tray. Any strong paper clamp found in office supply stores will work fine.

CREATIVE FLIP CHART STORAGE

Storage is a major problem, especially for presenters who do several different programs and use a lot of predrawn flip charts. After spending hours or days creating your training aids, you certainly want to protect and reuse them. There are numerous ways to store your pads so they are protected from damage between presentations. A number of commercially-produced units are available. However, you can save yourself some money and customize storage units to your needs if you are handy with tools or have access to someone who can do basic carpentry work. The biggest challenge most people find is where to put the storage units!

Let's first examine the commercial products available to you; then we will examine ideas for solutions you can create yourself.

Flat Drawer Storage Unit

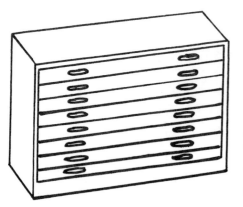

Flat Drawer Storage Unit

Large flat file cabinets can be purchased from many sources. Most are made to store commercial art-work or architectural blueprints or maps. They come in metal, plastic, pressed wood, and heavy-duty cardboard. (See Appendix C.)

Mobile or Wall Hanging Pad Unit

To store prepared pads vertically, try suspending them on a hanging unit. There are two basic types of hanging units. One is attached to a wall; the other is a mobile, frame unit with wheels. The pads simply drape across movable "arms" similar to multiple trouser hangers. (See Appendix C.)

Hanging Wall Unit

Mobile Wheelbased Unit

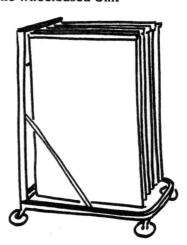

Compartmentalized Cardboard or Wire Storage Containers

Here is another commercially-manufactured space saver for stor-ing rolled flip chart pads or loose pages and charts. Rather than standing your mailing tubes on end in a corner and having them continually knocked over, you can insert them into a nifty little compartmentalized device. You can store your charts in cardboard shipping tubes for added protection, or roll them together into approximately a 4-inch roll. If you store charts without a canister, I

**Two Cardboard
Storage Units**

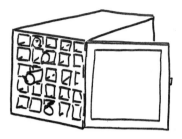
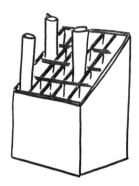

suggest that you put a rubber band at either end to keep them securely rolled. This will also help prevent damage when placing them into or removing them from the storage unit. For easy identification, write the name of the course or program on the tube so that it can be read without unrolling the flip charts.

An alternative when storing loose flip chart pages is to number each storage compartment, then create a wall-mounted diagram that shows which charts are stored in each compartment. (See Appendix C.)

**Two Wire Storage
Units**

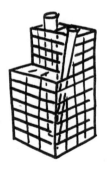

DO-IT-YOURSELF STORAGE SOLUTIONS

If commercial units are beyond your budget, there are ways to create your own storage solutions. They require a bit of crafting and some materials from a hardware or lumberyard, but they are not terribly complicated to build.

Wooden Frame Unit

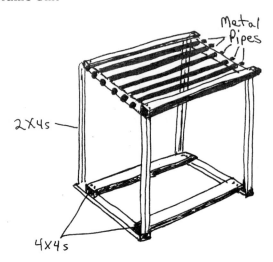

Wooden Frame Unit

Mount 1/2-inch (1.25 cm) steel or aluminum pipes on an assembled wooden frame made of 2" × 4" (5 cm × 10 cm) and 4" × 4" (10 cm × 10 cm) boards. All these pieces can be purchased at a lumberyard or home repair supply store. Use the 2" × 4" boards as a stationary base to balance the pipes and drill holes in them large enough to slide your pipes through on either side—and add the 4" × 4" pieces for stability.

Wooden Peg Storage Unit

Pegged Storage

For a pegged storage system, securely attach 4" × 4" (10 cm × 10 cm) wooden boards approximately 9 feet (2.74 cm) long onto storage room walls. Insert six 10-inch (28.5 cm) pegs or wooden dowel rods 1/4 inch (.75 cm) in diameter into the wood. (Or drive in 20-pound nails at a 30° angle.) Ensure that the pegs are spaced to align with the standard-size holes in commercial flip chart pads. When you are finished, use the pegs to hang your flip chart pads. Be careful not to put too many on the system, otherwise the pegs might snap or bend, or the base could pull out of the wall.

An easier alternative is simply to drive 20-pound nails into the wall at distances corresponding to the holes in the pads. The key here is to make sure the nails enter the wooden support studs built into your wall. The downside of this approach is that many buildings have wall studs approximately 18 inches (48 cm) apart, whereas most commercially punched pads are approximately 17-3/4 inches (46.5 cm) apart. You can remedy the situation by visiting the local print shop and using its commercial hole punch machine to perforate the pads at the needed distances. Another solution is to use large "bull clips" to hold the pads, then hang them from the nails. The clips can be purchased at office, school, art supply, or variety stores.

Perforated Hardboard

Here's a third alternative to commercial storage units. Go to any hardware or lumber store and ask for a sheet of *perforated hardboard*, sometimes called *pegboard*. This is the material found in many home garages, complete with metal hooks to support a variety of tools or other items. To prepare, first nail two supporting 2" × 4" (5 cm × 10 cm) boards onto the back of the hardboard sheet (one at either end), then attach it to a storage room wall. Use metal hooks, available at most hardware or home supply stores, to hang your flip charts.

A more costly alternative to hardboard is the commercial pegboard display unit, used in many retail stores. The display units support metal pegs, which in turn hold merchandise. You can obtain these in a number of ways. Keep your eyes open for stores going out of business, visit a local flea market, or order from stores or catalogs selling merchandising display products. (See Appendix C.)

Perforated Hardboard Storage Unit

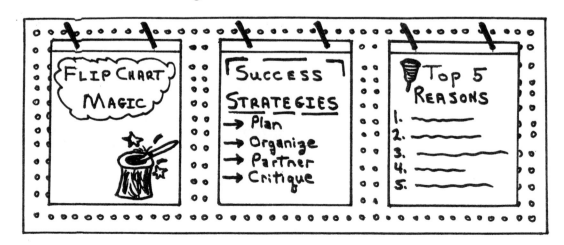

Tight Mesh Shelving

The rubber-covered, grid-shaped shelving sold at many home supply and variety stores is normally used in home closets or laundry rooms. However, do not let that deter you! You can hang a section of this shelving on a wall. Then, using a variety of looped hooks or merchandise pegs (available in home supply stores, such as Home Depot, Builders Square, and Lowe's), hang your flip charts from them. You can even use sections of coat hangers arranged in an S design to hold the charts. (See Appendix C.)

Mesh Shelving with Merchandise Hanging Pegs

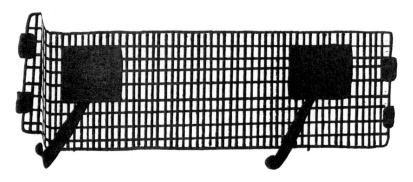

Slotted Angle Iron

Slotted storage calls for another trip to a home supply store. Once there, ask for a section of *angle iron*. This L-shaped metal bar can be attached to your storage room wall (either mounted on a 2" × 4" board first or nailed into the wall studs as described earlier). Once the bar is mounted, use commercial display hooks to hold your flip chart pads. Again, be careful not to overload the hooks or they will bend.

Slotted Angle Iron with Merchandise Hooks

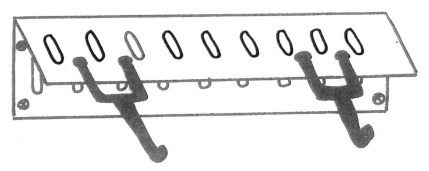

Slotted Wall Brackets

An inexpensive means of creating a hanging storage unit is to purchase two heavy-gauge steel wall brackets at a local building supply store. These usually come in lengths from 2 to 8 feet (.6–2.4 m). You can mount them on the wall with standard wood screws. However, since the weight of the flip charts could create tension on the units and cause them to pull out of the wall, you may want to mount them to a board first. If you are drilling directly into dry wall surfaces, use screws with expanding locking devices. Anyone experienced with mounting items on a wall can offer advice for your specific situation. Once the brackets are mounted, attach standard display hooks, also available at most building supply or hardware stores.

Slotted Wall Brackets with Merchandise Hooks

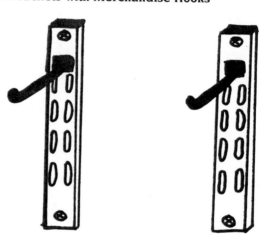

Part II

PRESENTING AND FACILITATING WITH FLIP CHARTS

Chapter 6

PLANNING YOUR FLIP CHART-BASED MEETING OR PRESENTATION

The key to making a presentation or facilitating a meeting and walking away with consensus, agreement, or an order, is preparation and practice. This chapter includes creative ideas you can use as you prepare flip charts for an upcoming meeting or presentation.

CREATING AN AGENDA

To inform attendees of your planned discussion topics, activities, time frames, and session sequence, it is always a good idea to create an agenda or program outline. At a minimum, I suggest that you outline the main events and topics—in the order that you anticipate they will occur—as well as the time allotted for each activity and when breaks and lunch will be given. I call this information *administrivia*. At the beginning of your session you can review the agenda for the audience, and expand on what will be covered in each topic. This is an excellent time to ask if the agenda items or objectives you have listed meet the audience's needs and expectations. If not, ask for participants' input and capture other issues or items on a separate flip chart page. More than once at a conference presentation I have had people come up to me at this point and say they were sorry, but they were in the wrong room!

You may want to post the agenda, along with session objectives on a wall. Participants can then reference it throughout the program, knowing what is expected of them and when they can anticipate a break. Knowing when the breaks are coming may prevent them from leaving the room disruptively throughout your presentation. I generally introduce this agenda as part of my opening remarks and ask participants what other items they had anticipated. I am always willing to modify the agenda within reason to meet the needs of my audience.

Administrivia

STORYBOARDING YOUR PRESENTATION

A technique I learned from a graphic artist friend years ago has helped me plan many presentations. It's called *storyboarding* and is used by graphic artists and instructional designers. A storyboard is a visual and textual outline of a presentation. It is a snapshot of what your program will look like.

When designing a presentation, I storyboard the different phases and create thumbnail images of my flip charts and transparencies. If you have PowerPoint or other computer software that allows you to develop handouts of your graphic presentation, then you have seen what a storyboard looks like. It is a series of images with written text about the program (key points, transitions, and so on) next to the images. You can use Post-it notes or sheets of paper to represents each flip chart page, so that you can easily plan and rearrange the text and graphics before you take the trouble to draw the flip chart page. I find storyboarding especially useful to help me remember to create flip chart pages for each key point I wish to make.

Even if you don't use the storyboarding technique, I highly recommend that you sketch out your ideas on a writing pad prior to drawing them on flip charts. This will help you visualize them and save expensive flip chart paper. When you are ready to go to the flip chart paper, use a pencil to write your text and draw graphics first to check spacing and correctness. You can then trace the images with your colored markers.

Storyboard

NOTES IN THE CORNER

Place "cheat sheet" notes in the corner of your flip chart pages to prompt you about upcoming topics. This is an old presenter's secret (although I know a lot of younger presenters who use it too). Lightly pencil in brief instructor notes in the upper corner (nearest the presenter) of the pages as reminders of or elaborations upon information that you will give. These comments can relate directly to the concept on that page or serve as transitions to your next topic or page. Such cues eliminate the need to use note cards. As you are finishing your comments related to the current page or are turning to the next page, you can look at the notes and start your subsequent topic.

CREATING IMPRESSIVE FLIP CHART DISPLAYS

Complex topics and ideas—for example, a mathematical equation, statistics, or a process that has a number of steps—beg for a visual explanation. This is where flip charts can really help. By spending extra preparation time illustrating hard-to-explain concepts or ideas, a trainer or facilitator can help ensure learner comprehension rather than frustration. A very effective technique for displaying a series of steps in a process is to put each step, along with bulleted details about it, on a separate sheet and tape the sheets in a row on the wall. You can then uncover one sheet at a time to reveal the series and emphasize key points about it. Once finished, you have a visual picture of the steps or sequence for further referral and discussion.

Overlays

To really impress your audience with the amount of preparation time you took, try using overlays when you have a sequence or series of items to present. The concept is similar to overhead projector transparencies. You have multiple sheets on a flip chart easel, each displaying one part of the sequence or process. Before creating an overlay, sketch it out on sheets of notebook paper to save wasting the more expensive flip chart sheets. When you're ready, use an Exacto knife or single-edge razor to cut out sections in order to "sequence" the information. Here's how it works:

- Count the number of steps in your sequence or process. You'll end up using one more sheet than the number of steps in your process.

- Draw your entire sequence on the last sheet of your stack of pages. The example below shows the five steps in the instruction systems design (ISD) process used by instructional designers. The "header" and all five steps are drawn on page 6 of our stack.

- Number all pages lightly with a pencil in the upper right hand corner.

- Place page 1 over page 6 so that you can see the process though the sheet. Trace a square large enough so that when it is removed, you see the header line only.

- Remove page 1 and place page 2 over page 6. This time trace squares so that when they are removed, participants will be able to see the header and step 1 of the process (Assess).

- Remove page 2 and place page 3 over page 6. This time, trace so that the header, step 1 (Assess), and step 2 (Design) text will be visible once the squares are removed.

- Repeat the process until you have squares that, when cut out, will allow viewing of the header and steps 1 through 4 (Assess through Implement).

- Now you're ready to cut. Stack pages 1 to 5 on top of one another so that the header boxes line up. On a surface that will not be damaged (a stack of old newspaper works well), carefully cut out the header box *only*.

- Remove page 1, line up pages 2 to 5 again, and cut the boxes for the first step (Assess) only from the pages.

- Remove page 2, line up pages 3 to 5, and cut the boxes for step 2 (Design) *only* from the pages.

- Remove page 3, line up pages 4 to 5, and cut the boxes for step 3 (Develop) *only* from the pages.

- Remove page 4, and cut out the box on page 5 for step 4 (Implement).

- There is no need for a page for step 5 (Evaluate), since once you flip page 5, you will automatically expose the final step of the process.

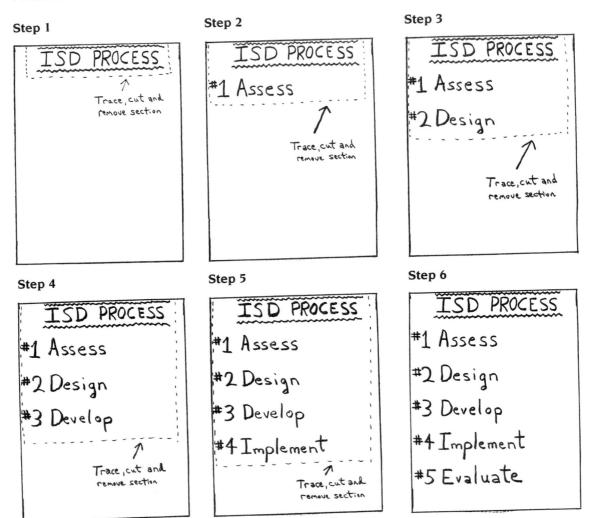

Wall-Mounted Displays

Here's another option for depicting a process involving several phases or steps. First, create a page for each step, then tape your pages to a wall in a descending stair-step configuration. The last phase is taped to the wall first, using a piece of masking tape at the outer edges of the upper right and left corners of each page. Then, add the next-to-last phase by taping it as you did the other page, but a bit lower so that the text, but not the title line, is covered for the first page you posted. Follow this with each subsequent phase in the same manner until you have all sheets taped in descending order on the wall. The first phase is the only one visible to participants. As you discuss each phase, move that page to another area of the wall, thus disclosing the next phase. Continue until all phases are disclosed and discussed.

To enhance this technique, you may want to post the sheets on one wall, then as you remove each page, have a participant carry it and post it on the opposite wall (starting to the left). I once saw a presenter ignore this guidance and end up looking a bit disorganized as a result. Halfway through his presentation he realized that he did not have enough room on the wall to add the remaining pages to those already posted. Guess where the flip chart for step 6 ended up? Yep—right there in between steps 3 and 4! The moral to the story: Think ahead and practice.

Pages Hung in Ascending Order

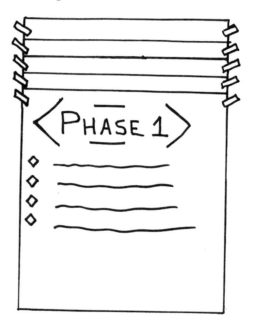

CONDUCTING AN INSTANT NEEDS ASSESSMENT AT THE BEGINNING OF YOUR SESSION

You will get more participation if you know what your audience wants and expects from you. One quick way to gather this information, while involving participants as they arrive, is to use flip-charted questions.

Before your participants arrive, think of a series of closed-end questions that can be put on flip chart pages. For example:

- How many sessions on this topic have you attended before: 1–2, 3–5, 5, or more?

- Are you attending voluntarily: yes, no?

■ How many years have you been with the organization: less than 1, 1–5, 5 or more?

Prepare six or eight of these questions and post the pages on the walls of the training room. Tape a length of string to markers and then tape them to the wall next to the pages. As participants arrive, ask each one to use the markers to put a check mark or other answer in the appropriate response area. As you begin your presentation, you will have a visual record of information about where your participants are coming from, and what they want from the session.

Needs Assessment Question Page

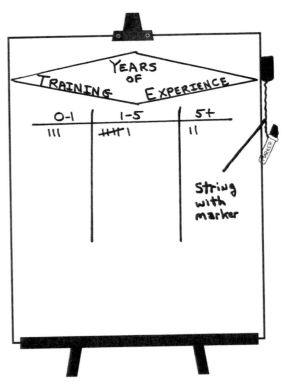

MAKING A ROOM LOOK INVITING AND EXCITING WITH FLIP CHARTS

Bare walls create a stark presentation or training environment. Changing that is a simple matter of advance preparation. If you are stuck in a bland room, there are many creative things you can do to liven it up and make participants feel more open and ready to learn.

Post Quotations on the Walls

One simple technique is to subtly introduce key points in your session by preparing several quotes in advance, and posting them on flip charts. There are many good business quote books on the market that can assist you. Search for some that tie into the program theme.

Once you have written the quotes out on flip chart paper or colored posterboard, add a border using a different color of ink. Next, add a graphic image, such as a bouquet of flowers, balloons, or a cartoon character. Do not get too carried away, but be creative and colorful. Here's one I use in a program on legal issues.

Sample Quote

Create a "Welcome" Flip Chart

For stimulating your audience and commanding its attention, nothing works better than a clever or humorous graphic image, a splash of color, or some type of creative accessory. Select images for your flip charts that relate to your presentation, but that define your personal style as well—have fun with your graphics!

One way to greet your participants, and add a bit of pizzazz, is to create a graphically illustrated flip chart cover sheet displaying the title of your presentation or program. For example, on a title page welcoming participants, in addition to the words "Welcome to…" you can add a smiling sun face, flowers, or whatever graphic image you like. These additions can create a warm, friendly mood while letting attendees know that you do not present information in a drab fashion. Also, participants do not have to look at a blank flip chart page as you introduce the program. Another benefit is that if you place the easel near the entrance, participants can be sure they are entering the right session.

Sample Welcome Charts

Use Flip Charts Instead of Handouts

A flip chart with the instructions for an activity (prepared before the session) can be simpler to make and more colorful than a photocopied handout. And it is always better than giving verbal instructions alone. Have you ever participated in a learning activity in which only verbal instructions were given? Chances are someone had to ask for the instructions to be clarified or repeated. By putting activity instructions in bulleted format on a posted flip chart, you make it easier for participants to follow directions. These pages help reinforce and clarify your verbal instructions.

SETTING UP THE ROOM

I encourage you to give careful consideration to where you position equipment, training aids, and participants in you room. Positioning can make or break a presentation. If you have been presenting for a while, you have no doubt occasionally found yourself in the wrong size room for a presentation. You know the drill. You have 100 people and the hotel catering manager sticks you in a 10' × 60' (3.3 m × 18.2 m) room. You could bowl in this room! Unfortunately, that is not why you came. The end result is that the people in the back cannot see your flip charts on a bet.

This is one reason I always ask how big a room is before I go to present. (Of course, I won't necessarily end up in that room after management makes its last-minute changes.) I also try to arrive the afternoon or night before to check out the location and, if necessary, try to negotiate a switch. Unpredictability is another reason that I prepare backups (i.e., transparencies of my flip chart material and handouts of the charts).

BRIGHT IDEA

Need to darken the room? Put several flip chart sheets side by side and chain them together from the back with masking tape. You can then tape these to a door or small window frame to use as a window covering (curtain) for blocking out unwanted light. You may need multiple layers if the sunlight is really bright, or you can spray flat black paint over the pages beforehand for an added darkening effect.

Improvised Window Covering

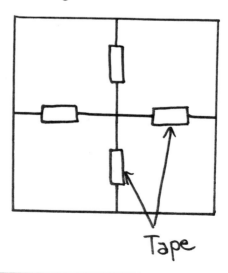

Tape

Assuming I am fortunate enough to get a room that meets my needs as a facilitator and my participants' needs as learners (it does not often happen!), I follow a standard setup that I have found successful over the years. My process is to set up the room so that I have maximum access to the items I am going to use most. Because I am right-handed, I position myself to the left of the instructor's table and overhead projector (when used) so that I can use my right hand to turn note pages and position transparencies. I then put my flip chart easel(s) to my left, near the wall. This allows me to write on the page with my right hand and flip the pages up and over the easel with my left. When I need multiple easels for small group activities, I pre-position them around the room so there is not a lot of furniture shifting prior to dividing participants into small groups.

If I am using a VCR and monitor(s), I typically put them to the right of the instructor's table near the right wall and out of my way. Since I always insert and cue my video beforehand, I use a remote control to start and end it. In this position, the monitor does not block anyone's view of the projection screen or the flip charts I will be using. In the event that I have a large group, I may put a monitor on either side of the front of the room (which means I then have to move flip charts to show a video, not a preferred option). Or I may place one on the right side of the instructor's table and one on either the left or right rear side of the room. I then ask people to turn in the direction most convenient for them to view the video. As I said, this works for me. If I were left-handed, I would reverse the order of everything.

BRIGHT IDEA

Ever gone somewhere to find that the screen you expected to use for slides or an overhead projector is either broken or missing and the wall isn't a suitable alternative? Try taping a series of flip chart pages together (on the back) and hang them as a makeshift emergency projection surface.

Ensure that your room is large enough to post completed flip chart pages and that it is all right to attach them to the walls. Some hotels and facilities will not allow posting out of fear of damaging wall surfaces. This attitude usually arises because some careless predecessor of yours did not use the right type of (masking) tape, placed pins or thumb tacks in the newly painted walls, or otherwise acted unprofessionally.

Also consider the positioning of the flip chart in relationship to any overhead projector and/or VCR and monitor you are using to ensure that you do not block your participants' view. The width of your room should be taken into consideration as well. Participants at an angle greater than 45° may have difficulty seeing your flip chart pages.

The bottom line on making your presentations effective is to remember the adage "You get back what you put in." If you take the time to follow some of the basic tips outlined in this chapter and book, your chances of a successful presentastion or training session can increase significantly. On the other hand, if you take a hurried approach and do not invest the time to handle the little details, they can derail your best intentions.

Chapter 7

Looking Professional at the Easel: Tips and Tricks for Presenters, Facilitators, and Scribes

Ever had an embarrassing moment during a presentation? You know, like when you are writing on a flip chart pad and the easel tumbles over because one of the legs isn't locked into position. Or when you are using a tripod frame and the legs slowly grow shorter because the locking nuts either were not securely tightened or have worn out allowing the weight of the flip chart pad to pull the whole frame slowly toward your knees! (Remember my easel evaluations earlier?) How about realizing halfway through your session, when you break and go to the refreshment area, that there is a shadow on your flip chart page and people in the back of the room probably have not been able to see your text thus far? The scary part is, no one said anything!

I have had many such moments. And even though they were embarrassing, I survived them—just as many of you probably have. Hey, you're even reading my book about flip charts, so I must have learned something from these incidents! I view these embarrassments as trial by fire for any trainer or presenter. It's going to happen. The key is to not let it become a regular event and let it rattle you. When something unplanned happens to me, I use humor. My comment to the audience after the sinking tripod experience was, "Look at that; even my easel is leaving. Must be time for a break." I then sent participants on a break while I addressed the defective easel.

To help prevent or reduce the chance of these types of events happening in your sessions, take some precautions and study this chapter carefully.

- Make sure that your easel legs are locked into position and balanced before you try to write. Check the easel before participants arrive to avoid the embarrassment of it collapsing in the middle of a sentence.

- Before participants arrive, go to various vantage points in the room to ensure clear viewing and legibility of your flip chart from all angles.

- Always consider available lighting—place your easel so that light shines on the front of the paper, not from behind it; otherwise a shadow could result, making reading difficult.

Properly Positioning Your Flip Chart

Incorrect   Correct

BRIGHT IDEA

Many presenters use a pointer to focus participants' attention on a specific item or area on the flip chart. You can add a bit of humor by using the rubber chicken—mentioned under equipment—to point to items on your chart. (See the Creative Presentation Resources, Inc. entry in the Appendix C.) Another option is to purchase giant-size props (such as pencils or easels in the shape of clipboards). (See the Think BIG! entry in Appendix C.)

POSITIONING YOURSELF EFFECTIVELY

I have a set routine when presenting. Here are some elements of my routine you may want to adopt for yourself.

- Position yourself on the side of the flip chart from which you can best write legibly. Typically, right-handed presenters stand to the left side (as they face the flip chart) and left-handed presenters stand to the right. If you are one of the fortunate people who can write equally well with both hands, your options are open. Just keep the next two points in mind.

- Do not block your participants' view as you write. They may be trying to copy or read what you have already written. To avoid this, practice standing to the side as you write. It's tricky at first, but you can learn to do it.

- Face your audience when speaking. If you need to write on the flip chart, do so, then turn to the audience as quickly as possible to continue your discourse. Try to avoid writing and talking simultaneously, since you're facing away from the audience and may be hard to hear. "Back talk" can be perceived as rude and may inhibit participants from concentrating on your words.

I once had a Marine Corps instructor who told us that he had been specially trained in the art of camouflage and concealment so that he could be "invisible" to the enemy. He said, "The problem I sometimes have as an instructor is that I forget that I'm really not invisible and that you can't see through me. If I'm blocking your view, just tell me to get out of the way." Unfortunately, some people are reluctant to tell you to move, so you have to be diligent about not blocking their view of the flip chart or other visual aids. Visuals don't work if your participants cannot see them.

Positioning Yourself

RECORDING RESPONSES FROM THE GROUP

It is important and helpful to capture participants' responses to your questions on a flip chart as your session proceeds. You also may want to capture ideas and problems for later discussion, evaluation, transcription, and referral or follow-up. There are several points to keep in mind when recording information during your program. These can help ensure that you are facilitating knowledge and ideas rather than simply pushing forward your own beliefs and opinions.

Always write down your participants' exact words when they offer a response or idea. To paraphrase or reword their comments without first getting permission or buy-in from them can send the message that you have a preconceived answer that you really want recorded, or that you devalue their thoughts. In addition, by paraphrasing without checking with them, you could be changing their intended idea or thought without knowing it. For example, in a program entitled "Introduction to Supervision," you ask for a characteristic of good leaders and someone offers, "That they be able to organize materials and resources and bring a project together on time and within budget." You respond, "Very good: planning and write that one word." In effect, you are cutting the speaker off. Soon participants may stop offering ideas because they feel you don't value their opinion or are going to capture only what you want.

My preference is to ask *the participant* to summarize or shorten a statement if it is too long for the flip chart. For example, assume a participant gives the response about leadership mentioned above. I might say something like, "If you had to phrase that in five or six words, how would you say it?" The participant now rethinks and restates. I do not run the risk of attempting to paraphrase, getting it wrong, and alienating my audience. Best of all, the response now fits on the page within the parameters we examined earlier for page layout!

A related technique for capturing exactly what your audience says is to tape completed pages to the wall for reference. If possible, ask participants to assist you to gain their active involvement, while you continue the presentation without interruption. Earlier I talked about techniques for effectively using the flip chart. Practice these (putting strips of tape along the edge of the easel for efficiency, tearing pages smoothly, and so on) and use them as you facilitate the exchange of and record information.

Many times, we get so caught up in the activity of capturing information that we lose track of our place in the presentation. One thing that helps me stay organized is to repeat a header on multiple flip chart pages, then put a sequenced number (1 on the first, 2 on the second, and so forth) on each page. Then, when all the pages are taped to the wall, the participants (and I) can figure out the logical sequence at a glance and relate issues or items. This is also immensely helpful if someone later compiles and transcribes the flip charts. One additional tip: If you are doing a series of meetings (e.g., focus groups on an issue), code the pages by session—session A, session B, and so forth. Numbering and coding can save you many frustrating moments.

I found this out the hard way several years ago when working with another consultant. We were conducting simultaneous focus groups over a period of two weeks. At the end of each day, we would give the completed flip chart pages to the client's assistant, thinking the notes would be immediately transcribed. When the assistant finally did start compiling, she had no clue which charts went with what date. It really did not affect the end result of the project, but it was a bit frustrating until we regrouped and figured out the system.

A technique that I like to use when recording information during a program is to highlight key words and issues—by underlining, circling, placing an asterisk next to them, or using red or some other bright color. I find that when I simply put words on a page and let participants read down the list, interest wanes. Recently, I found a new highlighting product that allows the lettering to show through it. Called Flip Chart Highlighter Tape, it comes in fluorescent yellow, green, orange, and hot pink. You simply tear off a strip and attach to your paper to add some color. You can also write on and reposition it. (See the trainer's warehouse in the Appendix section)

THE PARKING LOT FOR IDEAS

When someone offers an issue, idea, expectation, or concern that is not part of the planned agenda at a training or brainstorming session, I encourage you to create a flip chart entitled "Important Issues." (I have also heard this type of page referred to as an "Idea Parking Lot.") Tell the group that it is crucial to get through the planned agenda before addressing extra issues of concern. Explain that if time permits at the end of the session you will revisit items on the sheet. If that is not possible, you will either meet privately with people or schedule another meeting to address the items, if feasible. In this way, you recognize the importance of participants' concerns without sacrificing valuable program time or getting off track.

UNVEILING AND DISPLAYING YOUR MASTERPIECES

Once you have discussed the material on a page and are ready to move on to another topic, tear it off the flip chart and post it on the wall if it is for later reference. If not, flip it over the back of the easel so that it will not distract.

How to Turn the Pages of a Flip Chart Pad

I have seen seasoned trainers have difficulty with this one—turning the page on the pad! It's not that easy to do gracefully. If you have difficulty doing it, go back to the basics and practice with an actual easel. To flip a page gracefully, grasp a sheet of paper by the bottom corner closest to you—using the hand next to the flip chart. (Reaching across with the opposite hand looks awkward, and partially turns your back on the audience.) Flip the page up and over in one smooth motion. Practice several times before your audience arrives.

The Revelation Technique

There are times when I do not want my participants to see an entire page of text—for example, when I am discussing a series of steps in a process, or key elements of an issue on which I want to generate discussion around each point. In these instances, rather then displaying the entire prepared flip chart page, I use a "revelation" technique similar to that used with overhead projectors, when the presenter covers the text of a transparency with an opaque sheet, then unveils one concept at a time, To do this with

The Revelation Technique

a flip chart, I simply attach a piece of removable transparent or masking tape to the bottom underside of the page from which I am working—so that the sticky part faces away from the wall or easel. Next, I bring the taped area up and attach it just below the title line so that the rest of the text is covered; thus the page becomes its own cover. When I am ready to discuss a point, I move the taped edge of the paper down below that section or line.

Using Multiple Flip Chart Easels

Have you ever seen professional jugglers spin plates on top of a series of long, thin sticks? I am always amazed at how well they coordinate and maneuver between the poles, seemingly without missing a beat. I am similarly impressed by professional trainers and facilitators who have mastered the art of using multiple flip chart easels. It takes practice to choreograph several flip chart easels and synchronize them with other visual aids and the message being delivered.

The first step in coordinating the message on multiple flip charts is to *plan*. Plan what is to be shown and said and plan where to put the information. Part of this planning involves having a checklist to review, and to practice using the actual items before participants arrive. Multiple flip chart coordination is really not that difficult, but it does take forethought. I suggest that if you are planning to use several easels and move between them in your sessions, you use the same system each time. Also, follow a logical sequence or flow. Start to the left and move across to the easel on the right. I also recommend placing a large numeral 1, 2, or 3 at the top corner of each easel where it is clearly visible. (I caution you not to use more than three easels, since it gets too complicated.) Once you have done that, put corresponding numbers in your notes or lesson plan. The system lets you know where to look for information so you do not have to search for it as participants watch (and laugh).

To add a bit of variety, list the steps of a process in sequence from left to right on different easels. For example in a three-step process, the first step would be on easel 1 to the left (as participants are looking at them), then 2 in the middle, and 3 to the right. If there are additional steps, I would move back to 1, then 2, and so forth. A variation of this technique is to use the double-size easels now available from some manufacturers. These frames are large enough to hold two pads.

Using Multiple Easels in Tandem

Finding a Page on an Easel Full of Flip Charts

One common hassle is trying to find a specific page on an easel full of flip chart pages. If you have ever fumbled or seen someone else fumble in search of a specific page on an easel, you will appreciate this next technique.

For speedy location of an individual page during your program, try tabbing all, or key, pages. For flip charts prepared for one-time use, tabs can be made by simply attaching a 2-inch (5 cm) strip of masking tape on the front side of each page you want to find, then folding the tape in half and securing the loose end on the back of the page. These tabs should be affixed at staggered points in height or width (vertical or horizontal) and labeled on both sides for easy viewing. Write a descriptive or numerical title on the tabs with a fine-point marker or ballpoint pen to aid location.

Place the tape on the side of the page nearest where you will be standing as you facilitate. It will be less awkward when you need to refer to the tabs. You may also apply self-sticking tab-type identifiers such as those used on notebook pages. These are commonly found in office supply stores. In addition to tape, you can use strips of colored copier paper coded for different program phases, subjects, or key points. To attach the strips, use tape, glue, or artist's adhesive.

A commercial alternative to the strips are colored Post-it flip chart tabs. (See Appendix B.) These self-glued strips come in small packets that allow you to peel one off at a time and attach it, as you would a standard Post-it note. You may want to use these tabs for pages you plan to store and use over a period of time. Not only do they look more professional, but they also help color-code your pages.

How to Tear Off a Flip Chart Page

How many times have you struggled or seen someone struggle to tear a page from a flip chart pad evenly? Well, if it was you having the difficulty, don't feel that you are totally inept. It is likely the result of poor product design. Some flip chart pads do not have perforations (tiny holes along the top edge of the paper where the sheets are bound together). As a result, it is difficult to get the paper to start tearing evenly or to follow a straight tear line.

To aid in tearing pages off the pad evenly during your program, prepare your pages beforehand. To do this cut slits approximately 1-inch (2.5 cm) long and spaced approximately 1 inch apart, across the top of each page. Use a single-edge razor or artist's Exacto knife for the slits. If you lay the pad on a solid surface and press firmly, you can perforate numerous pages at a time. Of course, a simple alternative is to purchase pads that are already perforated along the top, then tear carefully.

By the way, if you ever hear of a course entitled "Flip Chart Page Tearing 101," please let me know. I'll be the first to sign up!

Hanging Flip Chart Pages on the Walls

Visibility is always a concern when hanging pages on the wall during a presentation. I have found that the best positioning is with the bottom edge of the page approximately 4 feet (1.2 m) from the floor. This will allow easy viewing by participants from the opposite side of the room.

A related concern is displaying pages so that the information flow is maintained. The standard presentation flow in Western cultures is left to right, or 1, 2, 3, and so on. I generally start posting items on the front of the left wall (as I face the audience), then move toward the rear of the room. I then swing to the right wall toward the back and move forward. Each presenter has his or her own technique; this one works for me. I'll explain my reasoning in a later section.

Note: If you are presenting to an audience from a country that reads information differently, consider positioning items and pages on the wall according to how that culture typically views or reads material.

TRACK THE PROGRESS OF YOUR SESSION WITH FLIP CHARTS

Flip charts posted on the walls are a great way to present a visual record of progress made in a session. Without embarrassing themselves or disturbing others, those who arrive late or who need to find out what happened in the meeting can refer to the posted flip charts. Ongoing participants can look around the room and see what has been discussed thus far. And a savvy facilitator can easily point to a specific chart or item and reinforce or refer to it throughout the session. Also, at the end of the session, the facilitator can initiate a question-and-answer game in which participants recall points brought out during the program. As the game progresses, participants can refer to the posted information as "cheat sheets." Finally, posted flip charts provide an excellent silent review for participants. (Such a review is impossible with an overhead projector and transparencies or a computer-generated presentation.)

GROUPING PARTICIPANTS

There are numerous ways to creatively and/or randomly group participants for activities and to get them moving around during a session. If you want to assign people to specific groups on the basis of experience, age, gender, or whatever, list their names in

Grouping Participants

advance on a flip chart, then unveil the list at the appropriate time.

For randomly grouping participants, there's always the stand-by (and rather dull) technique of counting off from 1 to whatever. Add more fun by finding out the number of participants scheduled to attend. Next, select some type of prop that comes in a variety of colors (e.g., erasers in a shape that ties into the program theme, such as telephones for customer service). You can also use toys in various shapes (cars, boats, animals, etc.).

Make sure you have enough props to designate even teams. For example, if you have 20 participants and divide them into four teams of five, you would need five each of four different prop shapes. After you gather your props, randomly place one prop in sequence at each participant's table location. A variation of the above idea is to use different-colored adhesive dots or stars (available at most office or teacher supply stores). Again, select enough different colors to match the number of groups you will have. Place one sticker in the corner of each person's name tent or tag. A third technique is to post flip chart pages around the room in different locations. On them you can write sports team names, colors, numbers, or whatever. Starting with the person to your immediate left or right, have the first person go to the first chart, the next to the second, and so on until all participants are in front of a page. You now have teams.

Still another technique is to cut out enough strips of paper so that you have one for each participant. Write the name of something (similar to the flip chart idea) on the strips. Pass these out to participants as they enter the room. Tell them that this will be the group for their first activity or throughout the day. That way, no matter where people sit initially, they'll be moving later.

A final technique, after you've determined the number of people attending the program, is to select that number of cards from a standard (or jumbo) deck of playing cards. For example, if you have 24 people in the class and you want four groups of six people, you would take all the 1s, 2s, 3s, 4s, 5s, and 6s from the deck, then set the rest aside. Since there are four suits in a deck, you have enough cards to assign six people to four groups. When you are ready for an activity, walk around the room and have each person select a card. The person's number is his or her group designation.

You are limited only by your imagination in getting people involved. There are hundreds of books and articles in libraries to help you. Also, I list training tips of the month on my web site: www.magicnet.net/~cprbluca. (Additional activity resources are given in the Bibliography in Appendix C.)

GIVING INSTRUCTIONS OR OUTLINING A PROCESS

Whenever you need to give instructions for an activity and want to increase the likelihood that people will "get it," try listing the steps on a flip chart in bulleted format. For example, if you were beginning a brainstorming session and wanted to ensure better results, list the "rules" for brainstorming on a flip chart.

Since most people listen at about a 25 percent efficiency level, the chances that they missed some aspect of your instructions are pretty high. When the steps, activities, and times are displayed on a flip chart page, participants can refer back to it without having to feel embarrassed by asking you to repeat. Such a

Outlining a Process

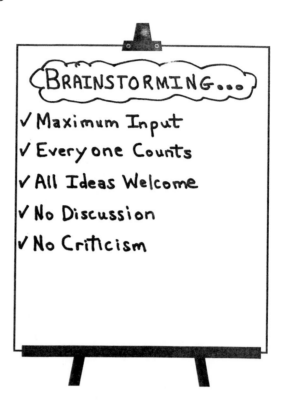

chart also helps when groups get off task and need to refocus on their assignment.

I often find that when I do not flip-chart instructions, I end up repeating them for individuals and groups several times. Most people will not ask for clarification unless they absolutely are lost. They typically figure that *someone* in the group understood the information. When this is not the case, the questions begin.

GATHERING AND GIVING INTERIM FEEDBACK

As Ken Blanchard says in his book *The One Minute Manager*, "Feedback is the Breakfast of Champions." Unfortunately, I see facilitators, trainers, and meeting leaders ignore the concept on a regular basis. If feedback is collected or given, it is infrequent and usually done in a less than effective manner.

To see what I mean, take a mental journey with me. Think about times when you were in a session and saw groups of participants interact in some form of friendly competition as they tried to solve a puzzle, come up with a solution to an issue or question, work through a case study, or whatever. At the end of the activity, there may have been a brief acknowledgment like, "Okay, team A has the solution. Let's discuss the activity as a group." There may have even been some mild form of applause or other acknowledgment. Then it was over, and nothing else was said about it.

Now think about a program where, up front, the facilitator explained the "rules" for the day while going through the agenda. As part of the opening events, the leader explained that throughout the session groups would be competing as teams and prizes would be given. The facilitator then creatively assigned people to groups, using techniques similar to the ones described earlier, or maybe even asked the groups to spend time coming up with their own team names. Possibly colored markers and flip chart paper were passed out, and teams were asked to come up with a mascot or visual picture to describe themselves.

Throughout the day the facilitator may have tracked team performance by assigning a point value each time a team completed the task, finished first, contributed a significant idea, or whatever. Teams may have even been awarded candy bars, buttons with phrases associated with the program topic, or other small treats. At the end of the session, they may have had a grand celebration accompanied by an audiotaped drum roll as the team with the most points was given recognition. And, so the remaining teams did not feel left out, there may have even been consolation prizes.

Can you imagine the difference in the energy level in those two rooms? The first program goes through the motion of motivation and giving feedback; the second creates an environment where feedback is built in.

Now, take the concept of feedback one step further: Facilitators need feedback too! How do you gather feedback in your sessions? If you are like many trainers and facilitators, you do so on an evaluation form handed out at the end of the day or at the end of several days for multiday sessions. These typically make you feel warm and fuzzy—assuming you did a good job and people liked your presentation style—but little hard data or comments are typically forthcoming. Even if there is some sound feedback, it is too late to make adjustments so that the group leaving will benefit. How can you remedy this need for and lack of session feedback? I suggest that you build feedback into your program outline. First, if you are going to use evaluation forms, I strongly suggest that you put them on tables before participants arrive and discuss them in your opening remarks. Suggest that people fill in comments (not numbers; those come at the end of the day) throughout the session as things occur to them.

I go one step further by building what I call "Interim Reviews" into my programs. At certain points, generally right after breaks and lunch, I have participants review material presented thus far. I follow this review by asking them to take out evaluation forms and write down one thing they liked about the program and/or content thus far, and one thing they feel could be enhanced (and how). For example, I might give each table of participants a flip chart and tell them to select a group leader and scribe. I then announce that they have 5 minutes as a group to list all the concepts, ideas, or themes that they have seen or heard in the session, or that they have thought of as a result of what they experienced in class. After 5 minutes, I have the group leaders share their lists. In line with the idea of positive feedback, discussed earlier, I then reward the leaders and scribes, and the team with the longest list.

What have I done? I have encouraged and rewarded participation. I have had each person review the material in a search for list items. I've reinforced concepts because participants have seen and discussed the items two more times (once as a group and once as a class during debrief). I've also gotten an idea of which concepts they thought were important and which ones I need to go over again because people did not get them the first time. Finally, I have recognized achievement by rewarding the best team at the end.

Following this review, I have the teams post their pages on the wall as a visual reminder, further reinforcing concepts. I then have each person take out a "Bright Idea" page, which I passed out at the beginning of the session, and write down one key concept to take back to the workplace to review or use. (Once again, participants are reviewing material and potentially reinforcing retention and learning.) The participants now have feedback, I have feedback, and we all are "champions."

Let me share another strategy for gathering feedback throughout the day using a flip chart. Before participants arrive, I use an overhead projector to project the image of a hand on a flip chart page and trace it. Next I write "Please Give Me a Hand" at the top and either spray the page with artist's adhesive or use masking tape to attach it to an easel, which I then place by the exit door. (The sheet is covered so participants cannot see it until I am ready to use it.)

Just before a break, I pass out sheets of brightly colored paper cut in the shape of a light bulb, (or something else related to the program theme) and uncover my flip chart page. I ask people to think about everything they have experienced thus far. I tell them to write down what they liked most about the program so far on one side of the cutout end to write what they liked least (and why) on the other.

I then send them on break or to lunch and ask them to stick their cutout to the "Give Me a Hand" page by the door, with the thing they like best showing. While they are at break, I review the sheets and, if appropriate, make any necessary changes to the program to correct the things they liked least. When participants get back, I encourage them to read the "best" comments. They are thereby reinforcing the concepts in their own mind by seeing

Getting Interim Feedback

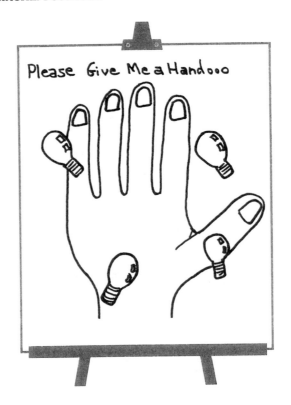

them again. An added value is that if the majority of participants liked something that someone has liked least, the dissenter may rethink his or her logic and make a switch. Also, if after I review the key points, it appears that the group missed something important, I can go back to cover it again.

Techniques like these are great for having participants review program materials and let me know if the presentation is meeting their expectations.

Chapter 8

FLIP CHART TECHNIQUES FOR FACILITATING MEETINGS

WARMING UP THE GROUP

There are dozens of books currently on the market that offer ideas on how to introduce topics, welcome participants through small group activities, and generate buy-in to program content. In Part III of this book, you will find a few ideas for icebreakers to help get you started. Also, some excellent activity resources are listed in Appendix D.

An added benefit of writing things on flip chart pages and posting them in the room is that participants are less likely to be intimidated when an activity is announced. Since people often do not listen to their full potential, posting information allows them to graciously read the instructions or visually see what you have just explained—possibly several times.

For example, to get participants to introduce and provide information about themselves as an icebreaker, I often write the items that I'd like them to share on a sheet of flip chart paper. As they go around the room sharing information about themselves, they can refer to the sheet so that they do not forget something requested. This type of activity is great, since it allows participants to start talking and gives others a chance to get to know more about their peers. One of the questions for this icebreaker might be: "What do you want from the day's program?" These issues can be flip-charted for later reference.

Introductory Activity Chart

SIX FLIP CHART ICEBREAKERS

I have found that, in most learning environments, people need a reason for listening and participating in a program. To give participants a reason early in a session, I have to reprogram their internal radios. My goal is to change the station from which they get their life experiences into station AVAR FM (Added Value And Results For Me). In other words, I have to give them a reason to listen by showing what they will gain or how they will benefit from participating. One of the easiest ways to show value is to get participants involved as soon as possible in their learning. There are numerous ways to do so, and with each one you can have people flip-chart their responses or ideas to share with the group. Here are some techniques to consider.

1. Pair participants and have them interview each other. Give them a list of things to find out about their partner and have them flip-chart the responses using a T-bar format. This simple activity gives participants an opportunity to network and learn about their peers through active involvement.

Gaining Involvement Early

2. Group people and have them develop a list of questions on a flip chart that they have heard or want answered about the program topic. For example, in a program on interpersonal communication, they might ask, "Why do people sometimes read into the nonverbal cues of others?" Once each group is finished, review the questions and either answer them immediately or announce that you will be discussing the various topic as you go though the program. By using this activity, you can uncover the needs of your group, determining what is important to them while getting them involved in the program.

3. Get participants involved in a self-discovery activity at the start of a session. I do this in a program on behavior styles. I group participants in threes, then ask them to write the first names of group members at the top of three columns on a flip chart page. Group members are given 5 minutes to think of three characteristics (adjectives) that describe their behavior. For example, someone might offer goal-oriented, assertive, and independent as choices. Through such an activity, people become actively involved early in the session, share information about themselves, get to know something about others, and begin discussing the program topic.

Learning About Participants

Maria	Phil	Shareika
Assertive	Persuasive	Conscientious
Confident	Outgoing	Task-oriented
Decision-oriented	People-focused	Traditional

4. After grouping participants, show a flip-charted statement related to the program topic. Have participants introduce themselves within their group, then discuss and flip-chart their thoughts on what they read. After a specified period of time, go over the group responses as a class. This type of activity provides a vehicle for discussion of a program-relevant topic, promotes active involvement, and gives people a chance to get to know one another.

5. Before a session, spray several pieces of flip chart paper with artist's adhesive and post the pages around the room. The number of attendees and groups will determine the number of sheets of paper. Also, position a flip chart easel with pad, markers, and masking tape next to each sprayed page. On additional sheets of paper posted next to the sprayed page, write an open-end question related to the program topic. For example, in a program on customer service, you might write, "What are some techniques for determining a customer's needs?"

Set Up Pages before Participants Arrive

Next, draw several different jigsaw puzzle images on pieces of paper (you can make each piece a different color to add pizzazz to the activity). The number of puzzles and individual pieces in each will be determined by how many participants are in the program and the number of groups you desire. For example, if you have 24 participants, you may develop four different puzzles with six pieces in each to have four equal-size groups. Cut your puzzles into separate pieces (keep the puzzle pieces together and do not mix them yet). Take one piece from each puzzle and paste it on a separate sheet of the sprayed flip chart paper posted on the walls.

You can now mix the remaining puzzle pieces together. As participants arrive, randomly give each person a piece from one of the puzzles. Tell participants that they are to go to each flip chart and attempt to match their piece with the one attached there. Once they find a match, they are to stay at that chart and wait for other members of their group to arrive. After all participants have found their chart page and the puzzles are fully assembled, they are to introduce themselves to their teammates and discuss the question that is on the wall next to their puzzle page. They can capture group reponses on the flip chart pad.

Here's a tip. After the activity, go around and collect the puzzles from each sheet and put them into separate envelopes for reuse. Your next program will proceed much more smoothly. Through this lighthearted activity, you give people a chance to have fun, get to know others, become involved, and begin thinking about and discussing the program topic.

Participants Try to Match Puzzle Pieces

6. Before participants arrive, place a page of flip chart paper and several different-colored markers at various points in the room. Once everyone is present, divide people into groups and assign each a project, question, or challenge. Allot a specified amount of time for the groups to complete the task on the flip chart paper. For example, if you are using teams throughout the session, have each team select a name and create a team graphic or logo. Once the time has elapsed, ask a spokesperson for each group to display and explain why the team chose its name and image. Follow up with individual introductions.

I like these types of activities because they give people a way to become active participants in their own learning. They also get people immediately thinking and networking. Finally, they help people recognize that the presenter will be facilitating their learning, but not doing all the talking.

SOLICITING IDEAS FROM PARTICIPANTS

All the professional, creative strategies detailed in this book can assist in making your presentation of information more effective. However, if your technique for facilitating and gathering information from participants isn't equally polished and professional, you may run into some resistance. Remember the adage "It's not what you say, but how you say it that counts." The same is true when asking questions or soliciting information. If you want to know something, ask a question—just make sure it is the right type of question.

Many presenters ask questions and get poor responses from the audience. This is because of the way they phrase their questions. Whether the questions are in writing or presented verbally, the key in determining the level of participant involvement is often how you phrase them and how you handle responses.

Two Categories of Questions

Typically there are two categories of questions that can be used to gather input from your participants—open-end and closed-end. Open-end questions focus on getting the other person to respond or open up and provide a lot of information. These questions often begin with a word like *what, how,* or *why.* They serve many other functions as well, such as helping draw out other people and get them involved in active dialogue. This is essential for a successful meeting or training session. Closed-end questions, by contrast, are designed specifically to elicit one-word responses (e.g., "yes," "no," "five") and begin with verbs (e.g., "do," "can," "will").

Too often, I have seen facilitators ask questions (typically closed-end) and get a sea of deadpan looks in return. No one offers any information or attempts to respond. To help overcome this problem, arm yourself with a series of good open-end questions to break the ice and stimulate thinking. Questions such as the following often work well:

- What do you think of what I just said?
- What could be contributing to what your coworker just said?
- How do you see this idea being applied in the workplace?
- How can we prevent this from happening again?
- Why do you feel that this occurs?
- Why would someone think or act this way?

Vote Taking

When I am facilitating a session or meeting in which participant opinion is desired I take a vote. I first list the challenge or issue on a flip chart, then have participants come up and cast their vote by placing a tally mark in the appropriate area. As an alternative, I may list the issues, pass out colored-dot stickers, and then have participants vote by placing each dot where they feel it is appropriate.

Vote Taking

Using Volunteers

You can get your audience members involved as individuals by soliciting volunteers. Ask someone to scribe (take notes) or capture ideas on the flip chart page as others offer them. You can have one person do all the flip-charting or you can ask for two volunteers and give each an easel. As ideas are offered, they can alternate with one capturing the first thought, the other writing the second thought, and so forth. This keeps the session moving along and frees you to facilitate and make comments rather than write. Another possibility is for you to work in tandem with one participant, in the fashion I just described for two volunteers. For the reasons we examined earlier, I recommend that you instruct the volunteer(s) to write down the ideas offered verbatim, rather than paraphrasing.

You may want to reconsider using the scribe process if the information being offered in the session is something on which everyone needs to take notes. In such instances, I recommend that you flip-chart the information yourself or have a co-facilitator do so. Otherwise, the scribe may miss something important. An alternative approach is to use a scribe, but have someone agree to share his or her notes with the assistant at the end of the session.

When using the audience participation technique to stimulate discussion and capture attention, I always prepare each question beforehand as a title line on a flip chart page. This facilitates control over the direction of the discussion, and keeps the subject in focus. It also saves writing time during the program. With the prepared pages, I can simply flip to the page I need and begin recording participants' responses.

Have Participants Tape Pages to the Wall

Another way to speed up the flow of a discussion or an activity is to ask a volunteer to help tape pages to the wall. As you capture ideas on flip chart pages, tear the sheets off and pass them to your assistant for posting.

HIGH-INVOLVEMENT BRAINSTORMING ACTIVITIES

Have All Participants "Scribe" for You

One technique I use to get all participants actively involved in a brainstorming or problem-solving session is to pass out 4-inch 10 cm) strips of paper cut from a blank flip chart sheet and a marker. When I am ready to have people contribute, I ask a question such as "What is one way we could better serve the customer?" I then instruct them to answer in a short statement and give them time to write down their response. Once everyone has finished, I ask participants to come up one at a time to post their response on a flip chart easel or on the wall. As they do, I have them spend a few moments explaining what they meant by their response.

Group Visioning Activity

To get people thinking about what they expect to gain from a program early in a session, I sometimes prepare a flip chart page in advance with the opening words

SUCCESS WILL BE:

Group Visioning

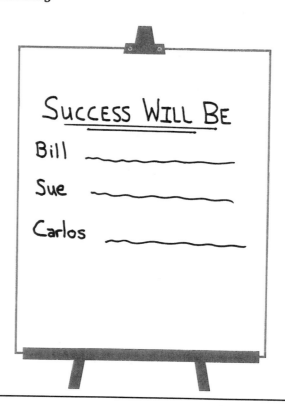

After I have made introductions and started the session, I ask participants to answer this question: "At the end of this program, what will have made the session valuable or successful?" I go around the room and solicit ideas, listing each person's name and response on a sheet of paper. I then post the page and refer back to it at the end of the session. At that point I ask, "Did we accomplish this?" as I go through each comment offered at the beginning of the program.

Problem Generation

Over the years I have facilitated many problem-solving and strategic planning meetings. Typically, to identify potential areas for discussion on a specific topic or in a session, I will prepare a list of partial statements on a flip chart page. At some point in the program I display the page and ask participants to finish the statements on a piece of paper. For example, in a supervisory leadership program I might list the following statements:

- The biggest challenge faced by supervisors is…
- One thing that would help supervisors better perform their job is…
- A key to helping motivate employees is…

After participants complete the statements, I usually collect their responses and review them with the group one at a time. Alternatively, I may form groups, pass the responses out randomly, and have the groups discuss them.

Mind Mapping

Here's a brainstorming technique for involving participants actively in identifying issues or possible solutions and structuring information. Tony Buzan developed *mind mapping* in 1991.[*] When done on a flip chart, it becomes a creative and visual means of gathering ideas. As with traditional brainstorming (see Activity 12 in Part III), some basic guidelines must be established to allow for the free flow of information. A simple mind map takes only 10 to 15 minutes to create. More complex issues take longer.

---

[*] T. Buzan, *Use Your Perfect Memory*, 3d ed. (New York: Penguin Press, 1991).

To get started, do the following:

- Set up a blank sheet of flip chart paper.
- Start in the center of the paper and draw a large circle.
- Write your problem, issue, or topic inside the circle—for example, "improved customer service."
- Tell participants to think about anything related to the topic.
- Draw a straight line from the circle in any direction.
- Write down a key factor related to the topic on the straight line—for example, "personnel."
- For every other item related to your key factor, create "branches" on straight lines connected to the factor.
- Continue to draw straight lines from the circle and add new factors.
- Work quickly and record all ideas offered.
- Do not get hung up with neatness, spelling, grammar, or other details.
- As in traditional brainstorming, encourage and welcome *all* ideas. No censure or criticism should be allowed.

Mind Mapping

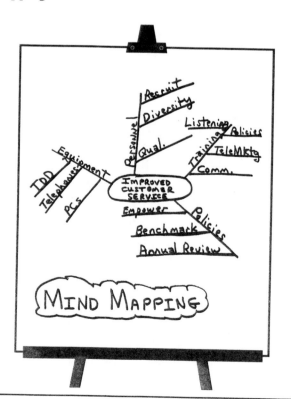

- After participants feel they have expended all ideas, set the mind map aside, discuss the topic in general, then go back and add any new branches or factors that surfaced.
- Analyze and expand the map after capturing all ideas.

Brain Writing

Another excellent technique for gaining problem-solving input and involvement, one that a colleague introduced me to a number of years ago, is called *brain writing*. To use the technique, follow these steps:

- Post a series of flip chart pages, with an issue or problem written at the top, on the walls of the room. Have plenty of extra paper and tape on hand.
- Give each participant a marker.
- Tell participants to go up to a sheet of paper and write one idea to address the issue or solve the problem shown at the top of the page.
- Once they have written a comment, have the participant move to the page on his or her left, read the previous person's comment, then add a second idea.
- Continue the process for 5 to 10 minutes (moving from page to page) or until people run out of ideas.
- At the end of the allotted time, pass out stars or colored dots and have participants place one sticker next to what they believe to be the best idea or solution for each issue.
- Tally the stars or dots and select the top three ideas for further consideration or discussion. If time is short, you may want to have everyone vote again on a single, best idea.

TRANSCRIBING FLIP-CHARTED IDEAS FROM A SESSION

Ever wish you had an 8-1/2" × 11" (21.2 cm × 28 cm) copy of your flip chart page for yourself or participants? With today's computer scanners, you can scan your flip chart page through the machine and produce as many small copies as you need. Of course, you can always do this the old-fashioned way, and type up the flip-charted ideas from a brainstorming session into your computer for later distribution. Also, some of the newer printers allow you to enlarge documents created in your PC and print them in flip chart size.

When you are participating in an ongoing project or series of meetings, you may find it especially helpful to capture information on flip charts. As participants attend subsequent meetings, they will have a visual reminder of what they did in previous sessions. You may also want to help participants create a list of meeting rules, to be posted at subsequent sessions, to remind them of agreed-upon behavior for listening to others. (See Part III for examples.) This latter technique can help ensure that agenda and meeting objectives are met. By referring to the "rules" that the participants created, you can help maintain focus.

25 FLIP CHART ACTIVITIES FOR BRAINSTORMING, ICEBREAKING, TEAM PROBLEM-SOLVING, AND FACILITATING MEETINGS

There are many reasons to use "activities" or "exercises" when training or presenting information. The most important one is that through such techniques where people become active participants rather than passive observers. They learn from their own discoveries as opposed to having a trainer tell them the answers. And we know that people are less resistant to new ideas they have learned for themselves.

The exciting part of placing participants in groups, giving instructions, and stepping back as they explore, discuss, challenge, and learn is that you as facilitator can gain new insights from their work. One of my greatest pleasures in being a trainer for almost three decades is to watch the "light bulbs" pop on in a group as people jointly discover a solution or answer to a problem plaguing the group or organization. In such instances, I am no longer the facilitator. I am the student being enriched by my "teachers." And I hope to continue learning for years to come!

To assist you in getting people involved, facilitating problem-solving sessions, or keeping your meetings on track, I have prepared 25 flip chart activities that I hope you will find valuable.

1. TAKE A STAND

Purpose   To quickly assess a group's opinions on a problem or an issue.

Objectives   This lighthearted activity allows participants to:

- Actively state their opinion or knowledge level.
- Move around.

Process
- Prepare a tally flip chart with these entries: Strongly Agree, Agree, Somewhat Agree, Somewhat Disagree, Strongly Disagree.
- Post flip chart pages around the room at different points, each with one of these same statements (or with a typical point of view about a problem to be addressed by the meeting).
- Read a controversial statement or question related to the meeting or session topic, and ask participants to go to the flip chart page that best describes their view on the issue.
- Do a quick head count and write the totals on the tally sheet.
- Present the next question or statement and have participants again move around the room.
- Continue the process until all issues or statements have been read.

Materials Needed
- Prepared flip chart pages with the preference statements indicated above.
- Tally sheet with all degrees of preference listed.
- Extra flip chart paper.
- Assorted colored markers.
- Masking tape.

Time Required   Approximately 10 minutes.

2. Can We Get a Volunteer?

Purpose To identify resources in a group, knowledge or experience levels, and interest preference levels at the beginning of a project.

Objectives Through this activity, participants will:
- Provide information about themselves.
- Volunteer to act as resources.
- Identify others with common interest, knowledge, and experience levels.

Process
- Prior to the arrival of group members, create five flip chart pages, each with one of the following statements at the top:
  1. I am willing to help on a committee or action group.
  2. I can assist with short-term assignments or projects.
  3. I have extensive knowledge and/or experience related to the key issue of this meeting (e.g., a volunteer activity, a specific business issue, a customer need).
  4. I have a little knowledge and/or experience related to this issue.
  5. I have worked on similar projects in the past.
- Once participants arrive, review the purpose of the meeting.
- During breaks, ask them to go to a flip chart that pertains to them and write their name. Stress that every person's name should appear on one page, but can appear on several.

Materials Needed
- Prepared flip chart pages.
- Assorted colored markers.
- Masking tape.

Time Required Less than 5 minutes.

3. Please Help Me Out

Purpose   To provide an action-oriented means of generating solutions to questions or issues from the group.

Objectives   Through a process of shared problem solving, participants will:
- Play an active role in problem solving.
- Contribute potential solutions to peer issues, concerns, or problems.

Process
- Post one blank flip chart page per participant around the room.

- Explain to participants that they have 5 minutes to think of an issue, problem, or question related to a given topic. For example, if the topic is enhancing teamwork someone might come up with "How do I get peers to buy into my ideas more often?" or "What techniques could I use to better organize my time on team projects?"

- After everyone has formulated an issue, give each person 2 or 3 minutes to write the item down on a blank flip chart page.

- Once all ideas are written, go around the room and have the author of each item explain briefly (in less than a minute) what he or she means.

- After all statements are clarified, give each person a marker and instruct participants to go to the flip chart page posted to the right of theirs.

- Once participants are in place ask them to rotate clockwise, writing one idea or suggestion for improvement on each page.

- Repeat this process for 20 minutes or until everyone seems to be running out of ideas. The reason for continuing the procedure is that reading someone else's comment may give a participant another idea or suggestion.

- Add flip chart pages as necessary when a chart fills up.

Materials Needed

- Plenty of flip chart paper.
- Masking tape.
- Assorted colored markers.

Time Required   From 45 to 60 minutes.

4. THIS IS ME

Purpose To help participants get to know one another on a more personal level and to increase interpersonal communication.

Objectives At the end of this activity, participants will:
- Have more information about their teammates or peers.
- Recognize similarities among participants.
- Feel a higher comfort level with their peers.

Process
- On one sheet of flip chart paper, list the items of information that participants are to share about themselves (see p. 147).
- On a separate sheet of flip chart paper, write these questions:
1. What did you learn about your groupmates that you did not know before?
2. Why isn't this type of information typically shared with others in the workplace?
3. What can you do to get to know coworkers better?
- Once everyone has arrived, instruct people to form groups that include at least two other participants whom they don't work with or know well. *Note:* You can also creatively group participants yourself to assist in separating friends or coworkers.
- Once groups are formed, tell participants they have 10 minutes to share the information topics listed on the flip chart.
- Regroup participants, display your first flip chart question only, and have people take turns introducing themselves. Tell them that as they do so, they should answer the flip chart question.
- After all participants have finished with introductions, unveil the remaining two flip chart questions and have entire groups give input.
- Encourage participants to use what they heard to strengthen and build relationships in the workplace.

Materials Needed
- Flip chart pad with easel.
- Assorted colored markers.
- Two prepared flip charts: one with items for participants to share and the other with three discussion questions.

Time Required From 25 to 45 minutes, depending on group size.

"THIS IS ME" FLIP CHART INFORMATION

Title/department:

Length of time with organization:

Place of birth:

Number of siblings:

Pets:

Favorite car/why:

Hobbies/interests:

Best workplace memory:

Favorite foods:

Favorite holiday:

Favorite color:

5. Not That Different

Purpose To help participants who may not work together see that there is often more similarity than diversity in a group and to start off in a light manner.

Objectives Through this activity, participants will:
- Have fun!
- Learn something about others in the room.
- Have a chance to introduce themselves to others in the room.

Process
- Tell participants they have 5 minutes to meet as many people as possible and share the information displayed on the flip chart.
- Blow a whistle, sound a bell, or otherwise creatively alert participants that time is up.
- Instruct them to group with three or four other people.
- Ask group members to determine, as quickly as possible, three non-job-related traits they have in common (e.g., like to cook).
- Have participants shout out that they are finished when their group has discovered three items.
- Reward members of the winning group with a token prize (e.g., candy bar, button with a program-related phrase).
- Have the group disclose its three items.
- Flip-chart responses as presented.
- Stress that we often are more similar than we realize and that through interpersonal communication we can better discover the similarities.
- Use this revelation to stress open exchange of information during the meeting.

Materials Needed
- Flip chart with:
  1. Who you are
  2. Your title

3. Where you work
- Assorted colored markers.

Time Required   From 20 to 25 minutes, depending on group size.

6. THOSE WHO MADE A DIFFERENCE

Purpose To prompt thinking about characteristics that make people successful in a given environment or situation.

Objectives By reflecting on past personal experiences and identifying characteristics or people they have known, participants will be able to:

- Pinpoint specific traits for successful people that they can emulate.
- Recognize what they value as successful.

Process
- Tell participants they have 5 minutes to take out a sheet of paper and write the name of someone they think was successful in a given environment or situation (e.g., managing others, giving feedback, listening, organizing time, dealing with change).
- Have them take another 5 minutes to list two or three behavior traits that made this person successful.
- Go around the room and have each person share the traits he or she listed and explain why they are important to being successful.
- Flip-chart the traits people offer.
- Once all participants have shared their traits, look for commonalties and discuss them as a group.
- Suggest that people think about how they can use these same traits for their own improvement.

Materials Needed
- Flip chart.
- Assorted colored markers.
- Paper and pencils for participants.

Time Required From 20 to 30 minutes, depending on group size.

7. THAT WON'T WORK HERE

Purpose   To get negative thoughts or obstacles out of the way during a problem-solving session.

Objectives   Through this activity, participants will be able to:

- Identify potential roadblocks to moving forward with an idea or process.

- Generate ways to avoid stumbling blocks to productivity.

Process
- At the beginning of a brainstorming, problem-solving, or creativity session, state the meeting objectives or present the agenda. For example, "The purpose of our meeting is to identify ways to increase productivity."

- Ask for any reasons that the objective can't be accomplished under present conditions. For example, if increased productivity is the issue, the reason might be, "We've cut staff to the bare bones. There's no one to take on extra work."

- Get all negatives onto a flip chart page and deal with them, then move forward with the meeting to prevent getting sidelined later.

Materials Needed
- Flip chart pages.
- Assorted colored markers.
- Masking tape.

Time Required   From 15 to 20 minutes.

8. Will the Mystery Guest Enter and Sign In Please?

Purpose   To give participants an opportunity to introduce themselves and meet their peers.

Objectives   By participating in this opening activity, participants will be able to:

- Share information about themselves.

- Learn about their peers.

- Laugh.

Process
- Have various flip charts pages posted on the wall around the room, with the letters:

  A–D

  E–I

  J–N

  O–S

  T–Z

- After everyone arrives, have people proceed to the flip chart pad that has the first letter of their last name.

- On the pad, have participants write their first, middle, and last names and the city, state, and country of their birth.

- Tell participants they now have 15 to 20 minutes (depending on group size) to get to know one another and share a humorous incident involving their name, place of birth, or life history.

- At the end of the designated time, ask people to be seated.

- Invite a volunteer to share the funniest thing that he or she told the group.

- Explain that throughout the session each person will get to know everyone in the room.

- Have people take turns introducing themselves so everyone can place a name with a face.

8. WILL THE MYSTERY GUEST ENTER AND SIGN IN PLEASE?

Materials Needed
- Prepared flip chart sheets.
- Assorted colored markers.
- Masking tape.

Time Required Approximately 45 minutes.

9. OUT IN THE OPEN

Purpose To provide a vehicle for surfacing issues or concerns within a group so that they can be discussed.

Objectives At the end of this activity, participants will be able to:
- Recognize their own concerns related to the meeting or program topic.
- Identify issues or concerns generated by their peers.
- Visualize issues by having them listed on a flip chart.

Process
- Pass out blank paper and pencils to all participants.
- After introducing the meeting program topic, ask participants to write down any concerns, issues, or questions related to the agenda or program topic. They are also to write why it is an issue or concern.
- Starting clockwise, ask each participant to share one item listed and his or her reason for listing it.
- Continue the process until everyone has exhausted his or her list.
- On a pad titled "Issues," flip-chart each issue as it is raised.
- On a second pad titled "Reasons," list the participants' reasons.
- As pages are filled, tape them to the wall and continue.

Materials Needed
- Two easels/paper pads.
- Assorted colored markers.
- Masking tape.

Time Required From 15 to 20 minutes.

10. SETTING THE DIRECTION

Purpose To review goals, values, or mission statements as a means of helping the organizations remain effective and globally competitive. Through this activity, you can guide others through a visionary process to establish, validate, or change the goals of their organization or department.

Objectives Through this activity, participants will:
- Examine their team and organizational goals, values, and mission statements.
- Make suggestions for any needed changes.

Process
- Make copies of the Visionary Worksheet (see pp. 157–161).
- After participants arrive, explain the purpose of the meeting.
- If goals, values, or mission statements already exist, display and discuss them from the standpoint of when they were written, their intent, or factors leading to their creation. Create a flip chart or poster listing these statements and leave it posted throughout the session for reference.
- Prepare a separate flip chart page for each worksheet question, to be used later during discussion.
- Pass out copies of the Visionary Worksheet and have each attendee complete the form to the best of his or her ability.
- After everyone is finished, have each person present answers to all questions. Discuss each question thoroughly and flip-chart responses before moving to the next.
- Summarize at the end of the session.
- Have responses typed or copied and distribute the summary to attendees for future use or reference.

Materials Needed
- Plenty of flip chart paper.
- Masking tape.
- Assortment of colored markers.

- Flip charts or posters for listing goals, values, or mission statements.
- Copies of goals, values, or mission statements to distribute to all participants.
- Pencils for participants.

Time Required   Approximately 4 hours, depending on group size and whether goals, values, or mission statements currently exist or need to be generated.

VISIONARY WORKSHEET

You are being asked to answer the following questions as part of our efforts to ensure that we are moving in the right direction as a department or team and organization. Think about each answer as thoroughly as possible. Your input and ideas are crucial to future success, so please take your time.

1. Who are our customers?

Internal (other departments); External (teams/individuals)

_____

_____

_____

2. What core products or services do we provide as a team or department?

_____

_____

_____

3. What core products or services do we provide as an organization?

_____

_____

_____

_____

4. What do our customers need, want, or expect?

<u>Internal</u>   <u>External</u>

_____

_____

_____

5. What value does our team or department provide to the organization?

_____

_____

6. On a scale of 1 (lowest) to 10 (highest), how successful are we at delivering services to our customers? (Circle the appropriate number.)

<u>Internal</u>   <u>External</u>

1 2 3 4 5 6 7 8 9 10   1 2 3 4 5 6 7 8 9 10

7. Why did you respond the way you did to question 6?

<u>Internal</u>   <u>External</u>

_____

_____

8. What new products or services should we provide in the future? Why?

_____

_____

_____

9. Which of our current products or services should we cease to provide? Why?

_____

_____

_____

10. What obstacles do you/we encounter in providing the best products or services to customers?

_____

_____

_____

11. What things facilitate you/us in providing quality products or services to customers?

_____

_____

_____

12. Write a vision statement for the team/department (100 words or less). Include:

- The team or department's reason for being.
- Things that we are.
- Things that we are not.
- How we measure success.

_____

_____

_____

_____

_____

_____

13. Write three to five goals for the team or department for the next year (or five years).

_____

_____

_____

_____

_____

14. How will customers benefit from these goals and visions?

_____

_____

_____

15. How can we get team members' support or buy-in for these goals and visions?

_____

_____

_____

16. How can we get upper-management support for these goals and visions?

_____

_____

_____

17. In what ways can we implement changes to make these goals and visions succeed?

_____

_____

_____

18. How will we measure our success?

_____

_____

_____

11. MEETING "GAME" RULES

Purpose To set meeting rules in order to provide a more structured, effective, and efficient meeting environment. These rules can serve as a basis for a more organized meeting and can be added to as the session proceeds.

Objectives By following these or similar meeting rules, facilitators and attendees can:
- Complete their agenda items.
- Stay on time.
- Reduce potential conflict and/or disruption.
- Be more effective and efficient.
- Keep the meeting positive and productive.

Process
- Create a flip chart with sample meeting rules (see p. 163).
- Post the rules on the meeting room wall.
- Discuss the objectives of the rules with attendees.
- Solicit additions to the list.
- Get a commitment to follow the rules before beginning.
- Refer to the rules any time someone violates them.

Materials Needed
- Prepared flip chart with sample meeting rules.
- Masking tape.
- Assortment of colored markers.

Time Required Approximately 2 to 5 minutes to explain and modify list.

SAMPLE MEETING RULES

- Do not interrupt others. Only one person talks at a time.

- Allow and encourage everyone to participate.

- Be on time.

- Stay focused; no daydreaming or working on other tasks (e.g., personal calendars, reports).

- Avoid phones or beepers during the meeting.

- Stick to the agenda. (Nonagenda items will be posted on another flip chart page for later action.)

- Respect confidentiality.

- Value diversity in the group.

- Come prepared to participate.

- Don't monopolize—give others a chance to speak.

12. BRAINSTORMING

Purpose   To identify problems and potential solutions or courses of action.

Objectives   Through this brainstorming activity, participants will:
- Identify key issues, concerns, or problems.
- Create a listing of possible causes.
- Generate possible solutions or answers.

Process
- Develop a set of brainstorming guidelines and post them before beginning the session (see p. 165).
- Review the guidelines with participants and stress that everyone needs to actively participate.
- Display a flip chart with the issue, problem, or concern written at the top.
- Answer general questions to clarify the flip-charted item.
- Tell participants how much time they have to shout out ideas.
- Capture as closely as possible the exact words offered by participants.
- At the end of the designated time, stop and discuss each idea generated.
- Have participants vote on their favorite idea by placing a 1 or a colored dot on the flip chart next to their choice.
- If no one item receives a majority vote, transfer the list of selected items to a new page, discuss the ideas further, and have participants vote again, this time for their second favorite choice.
- Once a favored idea is established, talk about how the group will "make it happen."

Materials Needed
- Prepared set of brainstorming guidelines.
- Plenty of flip chart paper.
- Assortment of colored markers.
- Masking tape.

Time Required   Various, depending on topic or issue and group size.

SAMPLE BRAINSTORMING GUIDELINES

- No criticism of ideas allowed.

- Quantity, not quality, is encouraged.

- Anything goes; all ideas are valid.

- "Piggybacking" of ideas is fine.

- No discussion of issues (do this later).

- Everyone participates; no observers.

- One person speaks at a time.

- Use inclusive language (consider diversity).

13. Nominal Group Technique—Coming to Consensus

Purpose   To encourage individual participants to (1) generate ideas that address a question or issue without undue influence from others, (2) present the ideas individually, and (3) discuss and vote on the ideas as a group. It is important to state the question or problem clearly and succinctly to achieve meaningful results.

Objectives   Through this activity, participants will be able to:
- Generate individual ideas.
- Select as a group the idea(s) that will be pursued to address an issue or solve a problem.

Process
- Prepare a flip chart page listing the Principles of Nominal Group Technique (see p. 168).
- Prepare another page with the issue or problem written out.
- Assemble participants in groups of 8 to 10.
- Show the predrawn flip chart page addressing a specific question, issue, or problem.
- Have participants silently and individually think of as many solutions or answers as possible for 5 to 10 minutes.
- When time is up, go around the room and solicit one idea at a time from each person; write ideas on the flip chart.
- Repeat the process until all ideas have been flip-charted.
- Post flip chart sheets with ideas on the wall.
- Discuss each idea to ensure that everyone understands it.
- Have each person vote on each sheet by number. (A 1 indicates the person's first choice of solution or idea; a 5 indicates the last choice). As an alternative, you can pass out five different-colored dot stickers to each person and assign a value to them (e.g., yellow is first choice, black is last).
- Once the vote is tallied, rewrite the top five choices in order of votes received on another flip chart page. Encourage further discussion on the value and drawbacks of each.

- At the end of the discussion, again have participants vote— this time choosing two or three.
- Rewrite the top choices, and discuss.

Materials Needed

- Prepared flip chart page listing the Principles of Nominal Group Technique.
- Plenty of blank flip chart paper.
- Assortment of colored markers.
- Masking tape.

Time Required   Approximately 2 hours.

PRINCIPLES OF NOMINAL GROUP TECHNIQUE

- Individual ideas become the group's.

- Superficial discussion or rushing to decision is avoided.

- Ideas are channeled.

- Decision making becomes more focused.

- Redundancy of ideas or discussion is reduced.

- All ideas surface.

- Each person has a vote in the decision.

- Group ownership of final idea(s) increases.

14. THE DEVIL'S ADVOCATE

Purpose   To provide a lively alternative for discussion after a nominal group process or brainstorming session has identified potential solutions.

Objectives   Through participation in this process, participants will:
- Become actively involved in the issue.
- Have an opportunity to share their viewpoints.
- Contribute to overall understanding of the issue, problem, or solution.

Process
- Prior to participants' arrival, write out the issue, problem, or concern on a flip chart.
- At the appropriate point in the agenda, post, review, and answer general questions about the issue without getting involved in detailed discussions or problem solving.
- Ask for a show of hands of those who have definite ideas on the issue and/or possible solutions.
- Divide the definites into two equal-size groups.
- Divide the undecideds, sending half to each of the groups already created.
- Ask each group to come up with a flip-charted list of points to support its position. The exact assignment will depend on the purpose of the meeting (e.g., problem solving, decision making, implementation).
- Depending on the complexity of the issue, give the groups 30 to 45 minutes to generate their lists and discuss.
- Set a stage for debate, with one group assembled on one side (with its flip chart) and the second group on the other. Follow these steps:
1. Anyone in either group can offer a point.
2. The first group starts with one of its ideas and defends it.
3. Someone from the other group rebuts the idea with a "yeah, but" response.

4. All participants vote on whether they think the idea is valid and merits further attention.

■ Repeat the process with an idea from the second group.

■ Capture each idea that survives a majority vote on a separate flip chart page.

■ Continue the process until all issues have surfaced, been debated, and voted upon.

Materials Needed
■ Flip chart paper.

■ Assortment of colored markers.

■ Masking tape.

Time Required Approximately 2 hours.

15. IDEA FACILITATION GRID

Purpose   To provide a structured, visual approach to idea generation or problem solving and involve all participants in the process.

Objectives   Through this activity, individuals or groups can:
- Generate a number of ideas or solutions.
- Visually approach a problem or issue.
- Create a written record of ideas.
- Add a feeling of concreteness to idea generation.

Process
- Before starting, construct an Idea Facilitation Grid on a flip chart (see p. 172). Draw rows and columns only; ideas relevant to the group's concern will be filled in later.
- Explain to attendees that the grid is used to visually capture ideas on a topic or issue.
- Announce the issue or concern by writing it on a separate piece of flip chart paper for ongoing reference (e.g., "What are the characteristics of an effective supervisor?").
- Encourage the group to generate key topics or characteristics for the top of the grid columns.
- Brainstorm ways to accomplish or address the topics listed (see p. 172 for examples). *Note:* If more than four or five key ideas are generated, create additional columns or annex flip chart pages to the grid.
- Assign each key topic to an individual or a group. Each group can then either implement the ideas brainstormed or develop an action plan for implementation, to be presented for discussion at another meeting.

Materials Needed
- Flip chart paper.
- Prepared Idea Facilitation Grid on flip chart paper.
- Assortment of colored markers.
- Masking tape.

Time Required   At least 10 or 15 minutes, depending on the issue being addressed.

SAMPLE IDEA FACILITATION GRID

Issue: What Are the Characteristics of an Effective Supervisor?

	A (Interpersonal Communicator)	B (Effective Delegator)	C (Good Coach)	D (Competent)	E (Creative)
1	Listen	Share meaningful tasks	Take time	Attend training	Be open to ideas
2	Provide verbal feedback	Communicate assignments clearly	Meet regularly	Practice skills	Think "outside the box"
3	Ask questions regularly	Don't "dump" unwanted tasks	Provide positive reinforcement	Read professional publications	Observe competitors
4	Provide positive nonverbal feedback	Allow adequate time for tasks	Share knowledge openly	Network with peers	Alter routine
5	Recognize diversity differences	Provide resources	Train employees regularly	Attend conferences	Read
6	Give clear, concise messages	Be available to assist	Set motivating environment	Consciously strive for improvements	Be persistent

16. WHAT IS IN A NAME?

Purpose   To provide a creative and fun approach to getting a group into the mindset for problem solving or decision making.

Objectives   Through this lighthearted problem-solving activity, participants will:

- Get to know one another.
- Participate actively in group problem solving.
- Generate a high level of energy.
- Start thinking from a problem analysis and problem-solving perspective.

Process

- Before participants arrive, set up the Name Game on a flip chart (see p. 174).
- Divide attendees into groups.
- Explain that in order to start thinking from a particular perspective, the brain sometimes needs a special "push" in that direction.
- Display the list of names.
- Tell participants that each name on the list is a word jumble for a particular sport.
- Give groups 15 minutes to discover the 10 sports from the names given.
- Ask teams to shout out "We did it" when they believe they have the correct answers. At the end of 15 minutes, if no one has finished, stop the game and verify answers.
- Reward the team with the most correct responses.

Materials Needed

- Prepared flip chart with names.
- Assortment of colored markers.
- Paper and pencils for teams to write out their answers.

Time Required   From 20 to 25 minutes.

THE NAME GAME

Name	Sport
1. Sabel Lab	_____
2. Yo Chek	_____
3. Bell V. Loyal	_____
4. Roc Sec	_____
5. Stan Symicg	_____
6. Sin Net	_____
7. Dract Kleinfad	_____
8. Rals Cose	_____
9. Graham Tonin	_____
10. Mick Clorbing	_____
Example:	
Gin Wolb	Bowling

Answers:

1. Baseball
2. Hockey
3. Volleyball
4. Soccer
5. Gymnastics

6. Tennis
7. Track and field
8. Lacrosse
9. Marathoning
10. Rock climbing

17. How About This?

Purpose To get participants thinking of alternative ideas, issues, concerns, or solutions during problem-solving activities.

Objectives By playing "How About This?" participants will:
- Generate ideas, issues, concerns, or solutions related to a topic.
- Become actively involved in the problem-solving process.
- Inject a little levity into the problem-solving session.
- Learn to "piggyback" on the ideas of others.

Process
- On a flip chart page, display the issue or question to be addressed.
- Explain the topic to be addressed.
- Tell participants that everyone will have a chance to add ideas.
- Have each person write several ideas to address the topic on a sheet of paper.
- Toss a Koosh Ball®, Nerf Ball®, or other soft item to a participant. After catching it, the participant should say "How about this?" followed by one idea from his or her list.
- Have the participant toss the ball to someone else not yet chosen, who repeats the process.
- As ideas are offered, capture them on a flip chart page. It may be helpful to have a volunteer capture alternate ideas on a second pad, since the pace may be quick.
- Have participants continue the cycle until all ideas from their pages are exhausted. If a participant catches the ball but has no new ideas, encourage the player to piggyback on one of the flip-charted responses. If not, the participant can say "pass" and toss the ball to the next person.

Materials Needed
- Plenty of flip chart paper.
- Assortment of colored markers.

- Masking tape.
- Koosh Ball® or similar prop.
- Paper and pencils for attendees to write ideas.

Time Required   From 20 to 30 minutes.

18. GETTING THE INFORMATION YOU NEED

Purpose   To use open-end questions to generate input, ideas, possible solutions, or comments from members of a group.

Objectives   Through this activity, participants will:

- Develop a structured process for use in brainstorming or team problem-solving meetings.
- To generate dialogue and ideas from the sample questions provided.

Process
- Before participants arrive, write each idea-generating question on a separate sheet of flip chart paper. Use the list provided (see p. 178) or generate a list of your own.
- Tape them to the wall around the room, using the revelation technique described in Chapter 7.
- After everyone has arrived, announce the purpose of the meeting. Explain that the questions have been posted to prompt participants' thinking and responses.
- Display the question sheets throughout the session and capture participants' responses to each.

Materials Needed
- Plenty of flip chart paper.
- Variety of colored markers.
- Prepared flip chart pages with idea-generating questions.
- Masking tape.

Time Required   From 1 hour to several, depending on the purpose of the meeting.

SAMPLE IDEA-GENERATING QUESTIONS

■ Who will be affected by or benefit from _____ (changes we are considering, new process we are implementing)?

■ From whom are we likely to have resistance (support)?

■ In what ways can we increase _____ (productivity, finance levels, investments, morale)?

■ What is the most efficient way to _____ (implement the new _____ system, recognize customer needs)?

■ When does _____ typically occur (breakdown in the equipment, lower morale, customer dissatisfaction)?

■ When should we _____ (approach upper management, make the announcement, start the process)?

■ Where can we _____ (find support for the idea, get additional resources, go for more information)?

■ Where are we most likely to encounter _____ (delays, frustration, support, resistance)?

■ Why is this change important (insignificant)?

■ Why have we been able (unable) to _____ (gain commitment, reach our goal, satisfy needs)?

■ On the basis of what we know about _____, how can we improve _____ (service, quality, product distribution)?

■ How can we better _____ (analyze needs, position the organization to be competitive)?

■ In what ways can we better market _____ (our ideas, the new products, our program or services)?

19. THAT'S A GOOD QUESTION

Purpose   To use preplanned questions to stimulate discussion and ideas on a topic.

Objectives   By answering prepared questions, participants will:
- Generate new ideas.
- Establish a creative atmosphere for the exchange of ideas.
- Participate actively in the brainstorming process.

Process
- Develop a list of questions pertaining to the topic or issue addressed by the meeting or program (e.g., "What are the goals of our organization?").
- Write each question at the top of a flip chart page.
- If current answers to the question already exist, write them on a separate flip chart page.
- Display one question at a time and ask participants to brainstorm (see the sample rules for brainstorming in Activity 12).
- As responses are offered, write them on the flip chart page. Use the attendees' actual words when possible. (If space is limited, get permission to condense participants' words so as not to discount what they have said.)
- After attendees have run out of ideas, display the established responses so participants can compare their answers with existing ideas. An alternative is to provide preexisting issues first to serve as a baseline for discussion.

Materials Needed
- Preplanned questions, each on a separate flip chart page.
- List of established responses, if any.
- Plenty of flip chart paper.
- Assorted colored markers.
- Masking tape.

Time Required   Varies, depending on the number of questions used.

20. I Question That

Purpose   To encourage attendees at a problem-solving session to ask questions that will prompt the generation of new ideas or uncover potential obstacles.

Objectives   By participating in this activity, attendees will:
- Become actively involved in the problem-solving process.
- Generate a list of questions from which they can create potential solutions.

Process
- Group participants into equal-size teams.
- Pass out blank flip chart pages and markers to each group.
- Have each team generate as many questions as possible related to the issue being addressed in the meeting (see p. 181).
- Encourage participants to think of the issue first from a broad perspective (e.g., organizationally, industrywide, customers as a whole), then focus more finitely (e.g., department or team, specific customer or type of customer).
- Tell groups they have 30 minutes to work out their questions on scrap paper.
- Transfer each group's list of questions to a flip chart page.
- After all questions are captured, have each group share its list with others.
- Comment on questions as appropriate.

Materials Needed
- Flip chart paper.
- Assorted colored markers.
- Masking tape.

Time Required   From 60 to 90 minutes.

SAMPLE QUESTIONS

Issue: In What Ways Can We Prepare to Compete in the 21st Century?

Broad
- In what ways are we different from the competition?
- In what ways are we similar to the competition?
- In what ways can we increase our output?
- In what ways can we increase the quality of our product or service?
- In what ways can we appeal to a broader customer base?
- In what ways can we better promote our product or service?

Finite
- How does our department fare in competing in the marketplace?
- How can we increase departmental efficiency?
- How can we as a team enhance the quality of our services?
- How can our team add more value to the organization?
- What can we do at the departmental level to better address customer needs?

21. You Are Next

Purpose   To actively involve meeting participants in discussion, problem solving, or idea creation.

Objectives   By using a process of shared facilitation, participants will:

- Become involved in the idea generation process.
- Engage in an active environment for exchanging ideas.
- Generate ideas or problem solutions creatively.
- Depart from meeting monotony.

Process
- Before the meeting, place cardboard name tents at each participant location.
- Randomly put a number (1 through total number of attendees) on each name tent.
- Introduce the meeting or training topic and provide appropriate background information and/or handouts.
- Encourage each person to think of one question or item related to the topic, issue, or problem.
- Ask the attendee with name tent number 1 to come up to the easel and write his or her question at the top of the page.
- Encourage the remaining participants to generate responses. Have volunteers step forward to write responses on the page.
- Once a page is full of responses, remove it and tape it to the wall.
- Ask attendee number 2 to come to come to the easel and write a question. Continue until all participants have facilitated.
- Debrief the activity by adding pertinent items or questions that have not been addressed.

Materials Needed
- Plenty of flip chart paper.
- Assorted colored markers.
- Masking tape.
- Handouts as appropriate.

Time Required   From 60 to 90 minutes for a group of five to eight attendees.

22. CHOOSE YOUR TOPIC

Purpose   To bring a different approach to problem solving or idea generation to a training program or team meeting.

Objectives   By thinking through prepared questions or topics, participants will:

- Become actively involved in generating ideas, solutions, or concerns.
- Create idea or solution lists that are directly related to the meeting or training topic.
- Engage in group discussion.

Process
- Before the meeting, create flip chart pages with questions, issues, or problems (one item per page).
- Tape the pages to the wall at various locations in the room.
- Place assorted colored markers and strips of masking tape next to each posted page.
- As participants arrive, creatively assign them to a group using colored dots on name tags, a variety of toy props, or some other random system.
- Assign each group to a flip-charted page.
- Tell groups they have 10 minutes to create a list of responses to the issue written on their page.
- When time is up, blow a whistle, play music, or signal the end in some other manner.
- Ask groups to rotate counterclockwise to the next page and repeat the process.
- Continue until all groups have visited each page.
- Go through each page, asking groups for clarification of a point or for additional feedback on how or why the point is important.

Materials Needed
- Plenty of flip chart paper.
- Assorted colored markers.
- Masking tape.

Time Required   At least 10 minutes per page, as well as time to introduce and debrief the activity.

23. WHAT I KNOW

Purpose   To identify and build on current levels of participant knowledge at a training session or team building meeting.

Objectives   Through this interactive process, participants will:
- Display their current knowledge related to the meeting or training topic.
- Analyze what they currently know about the meeting topic.
- Become actively involved in the idea-generating process.

Process
- Create a flip-chart page listing the key topic to be addressed (see p.187). Provide a copy for each group.
- Create handouts of the sample grid for groups to use as a guide.
- Post the prepared flip chart pages around the room. Leave enough space between locations so groups can meet and discuss without disturbing one another.
- Spray each flip chart grid with artists' adhesive.
- From white posterboard, cut out small squares the same size as those on the grid of the predrawn flip charts. Prepare a complete set (with enough squares to cover the grid) for each group.
- On the front side of each card, write features, factors, or characteristics related to the key topic listed on the flip chart page (see p. 187).
- Divide attendees into equal-size groups.
- Place one set of cards in an envelope for each group.
- Have each group select a leader or spokesperson.
- Ask groups to open their envelopes and take 5 minutes to place the cards under the appropriate grid columns.
- After 5 minutes, call "time" and have the groups stop where they are.
- Have each spokesperson explain the group's decision on where to position the squares.

- Encourage other groups to offer input or differing perspectives.

- Assign each group a column topic. Ask the groups to take 30 minutes to discuss the value of each item shown on the cards. They are also to generate a list of alternatives or other ideas about each item. Have them flip-chart their ideas on a separate sheet of paper.

- Debrief the activity by having each group explain its list of alternatives. Add and encourage appropriate comments.

Materials Needed

- One predrawn flip chart grid for each group.
- Plenty of flip chart paper.
- Assorted colored markers.
- Masking tape.
- Artist's adhesive spray.
- White posterboard cut into squares.
- Envelopes.
- Handouts of the sample grid to use as a guideline.

Time Required From 1 to 2 hours, depending on the number of groups.

SAMPLE "WHAT I KNOW" GRID
Topic: What Determines Customer Satisfaction

Product	Service	Employees	Organization	Customer
Quality	Availability	Attitude	Policy	Attitude
Availability	Timeliness	Knowledge	Degree of management support	Available time
Comparable value	Quality	Helpfulness	Name recognition	Perceived needs
Warranty	Level of decision making	Availability	Reputation	Past experiences
Accessories	Follow-up	Willingness to assist	Location(s)	Knowledge about product or service
Degree of user-friendliness	Follow-through	Degree of decision-making empowerment	Advertising	Preferred behavioral style

24. One Minute of Praise

Purpose To encourage individual participation in a day-long meeting and to give each member positive feedback on his or her performance.

Objectives At the end of this activity, participants will:
- Feel good about their performance during the meeting.
- Be able to practice their feedback skills with their peers.

Process
- Before participants arrive, create a flip chart page for each participant. Leave the pages on the easel.
- At the beginning of the meeting, stress that everyone's input is crucial. Note that, to encourage participation, each person will receive feedback throughout the day.
- Instruct participants that you have prepared a stack of feedback sheets with each person's name at the top. During breaks and at the end of the day, they are to come to the easel and provide written feedback on something they liked about each person's performance. For example, "I appreciated the fact that you arrived on time and returned punctually from breaks," or "I liked the way you didn't back down on the productivity issue."
- Throughout the day before breaks and lunch, remind everyone to comment on each sheet.
- At the end of the day, give sheets with comments to each person.

Note: To ensure that everyone gets at least one positive "stroke," enter your own comments on the sheets throughout the day.

Materials Needed
- Flip chart pages for each participant.
- Assorted colored markers.

Time Required No extra time needed. The activity is completed during breaks or lunch.

25. WORD SEARCH REVIEW

Purpose   To energize participants (in a group with a maximum of 18 people) midway through a training session, and to emphasize key issues covered to that point.

Objectives   Through an interactive team activity, participants will:

- Review key points presented.
- Work together to compete against other groups.
- Practice intragroup communications.
- Have fun!

Process
- Prepare a Word Search flipchart with key words, ideas, and concepts hidden and scattered among the series of letters (see p. 191). Provide a separate chart for each group.
- On a separate flip chart page for each group, list the hidden words alphabetically as clues.
- Divide participants into three equal-size teams.
- When participants are ready for an interim review during the program, unveil the two sets of prepared flip charts.
- Have each team line up in a row before an easel containing the scrambled words.
- Explain that words can be found across, backward, up, down, or diagonally.
- Proceed with the game as follows.
1. At your signal, the first person in each team steps up to the flip chart to try to locate one of the clue words.
2. Once a word is found, the player circles it, rushes back to the team, passes the marker to the next person, and goes to the end of the line.
3. The second player continues the cycle.
4. The team getting all the terms first shouts "Done." All other teams stop looking for words.
- Verify the results. If all terms have been found, reward the winners (with small tokens, candy bars, and so on).

- If words have been missed, shout "Continue" and have teams resume play until someone again yells "Done." The verification process is repeated.
- Review the key terms and definitions as a group.

Materials Needed

- Prepared Word Search sheets.
- Prepared sheets with word clues.
- Assorted colored markers.
- Incentive rewards.
- Easels, or masking tape to attach paper to the wall.

Time Required   Approximately 10 minutes.

SAMPLE WORD SEARCH
Topic: Supervisor Role Review

```
F C O U N S E L O R A Z J I M O L T
A B J L D E C I S I O N M A K E R S
S S I R E B V A H E M I O P I S E Q
D T W P L A N N E R G Y T V K M S E
B M U K E S Y J S P A G I T N C O A
T O T V G P O U M N Z K V K O N U I
J C R E A T I V E V Y M A Y I A R P
O O E J T H B X N S M S T H Z E C H
Y M S P O L K R T I Y F O B N O E N
U M I L R T O B O P X Y R I E N M I
K U V E D E M A R E K H A Z T P A M
L N D I O R S L A N J R L F A N N X
E I A C A X N O P G T I Z V A L A C
M C O A C H M W U J T O K L O M G W
F A G M T Q V O K R A B Y C X Y E G
Z T F L Y A H B Z I C S P O U T R A
H O T O R I S B T E T E D A W L L O
O R E K A T K S I R E P O C M E Y P
```

ADVISER
ANALYST
COACH
COMMUNICATOR
COUNSELOR

CREATIVE
DECISION MAKER
DELEGATOR
MENTOR
MOTIVATOR

PLANNER
RESOURCE
RESOURCE MANAGER
RISK TAKER
TRAINER

APPENDIXES

50 Simple, Ready to Use Template Flip Charts,
to Impress Participants
When They Walk into the Room

ACTION STICK FIGURES

ACTION STAR FIGURES

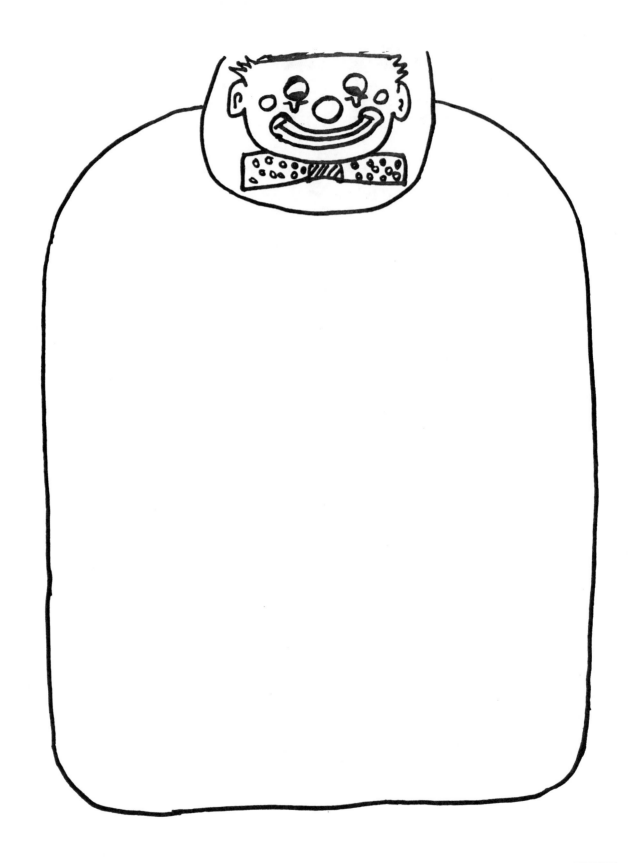

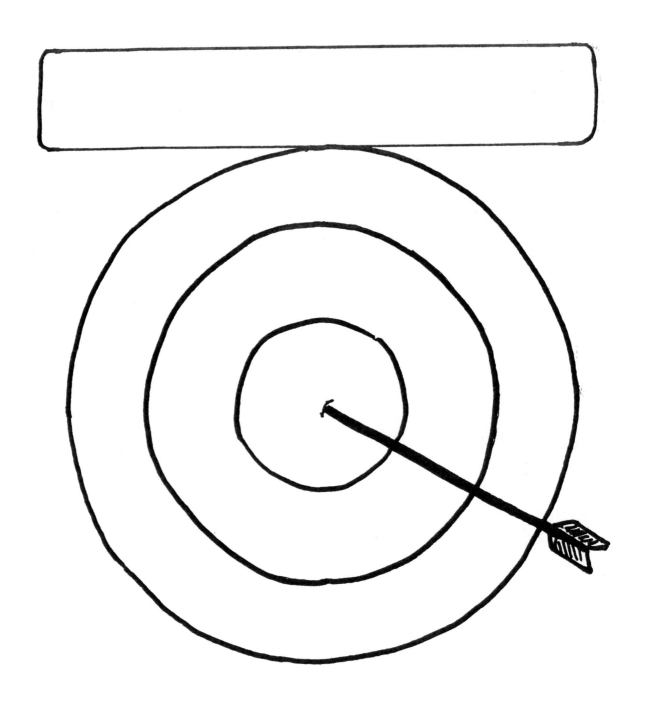

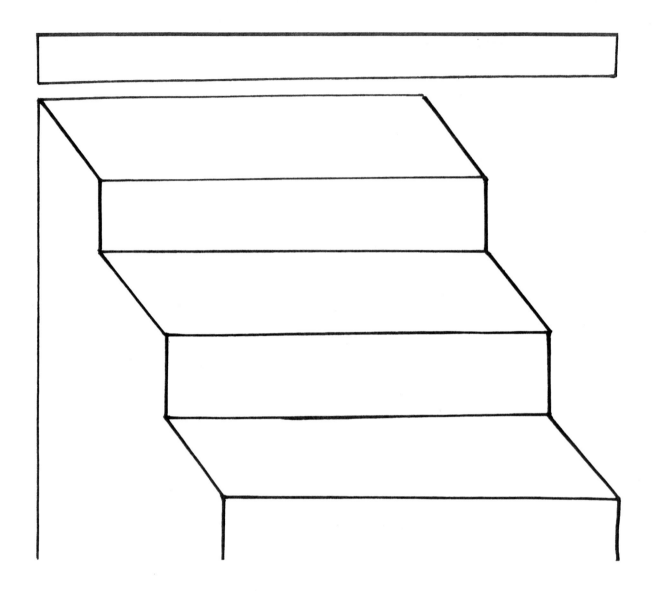

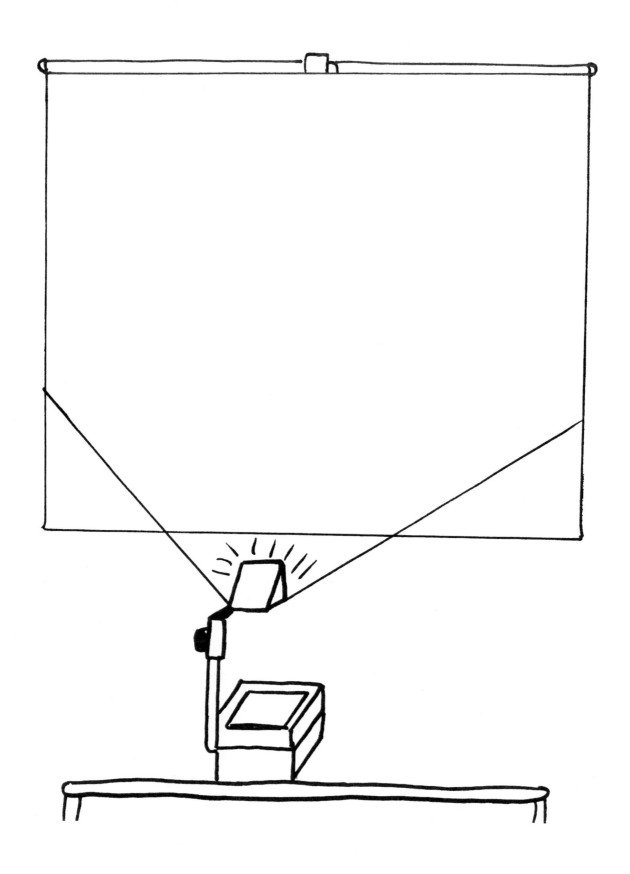

Welcome!!

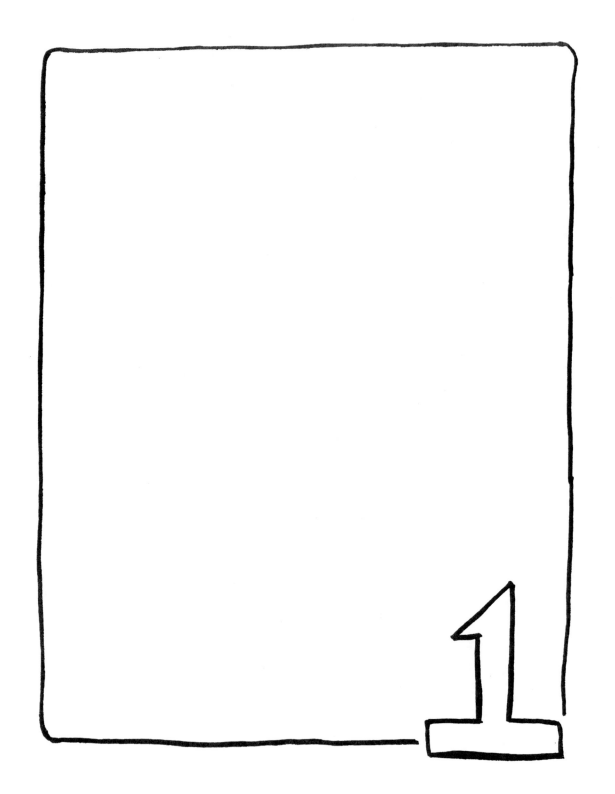

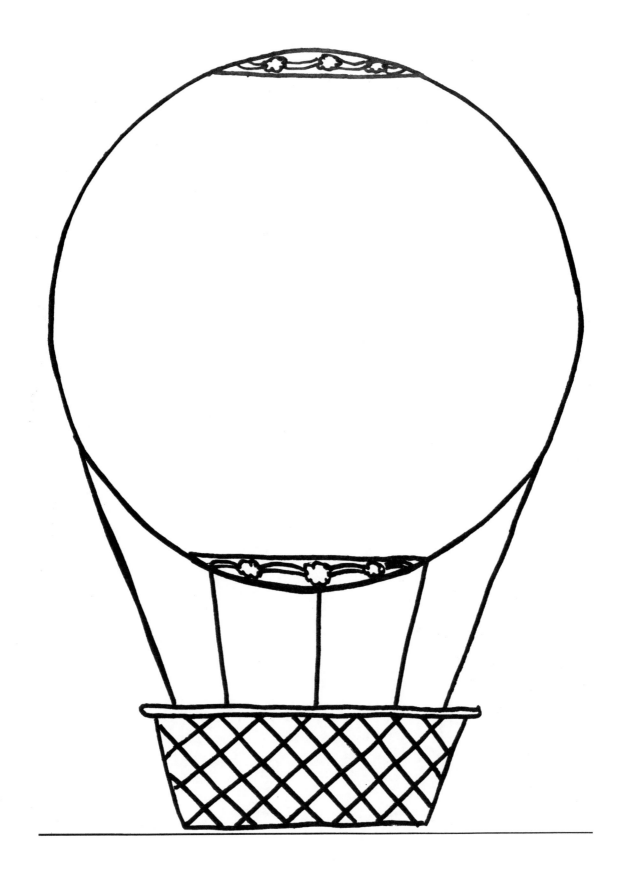

Welcome To

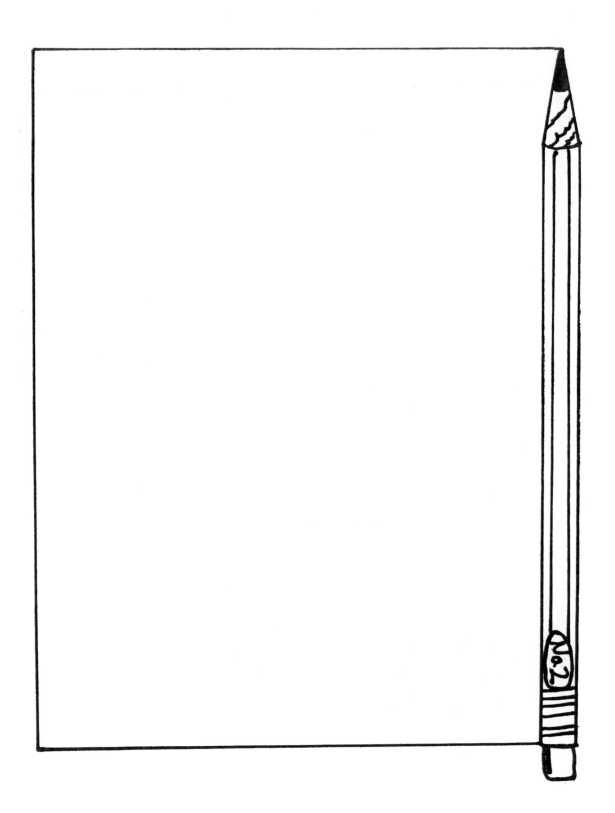

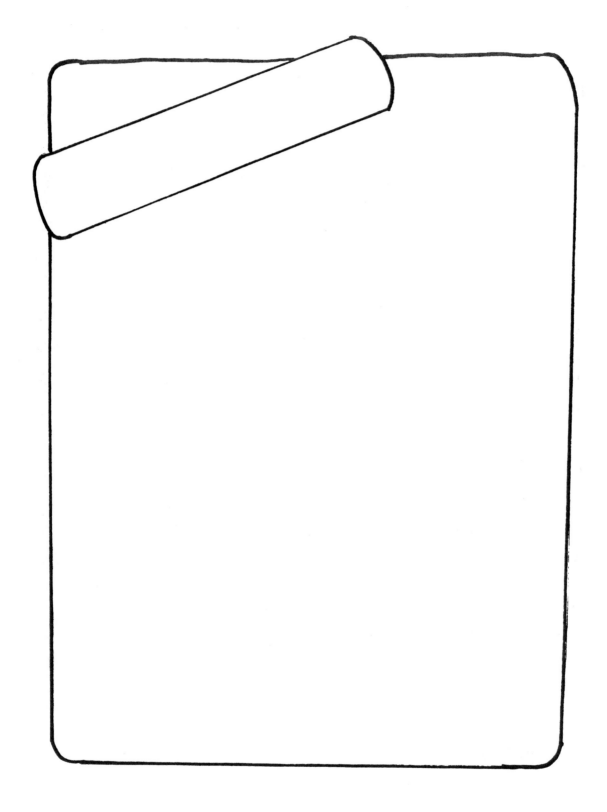

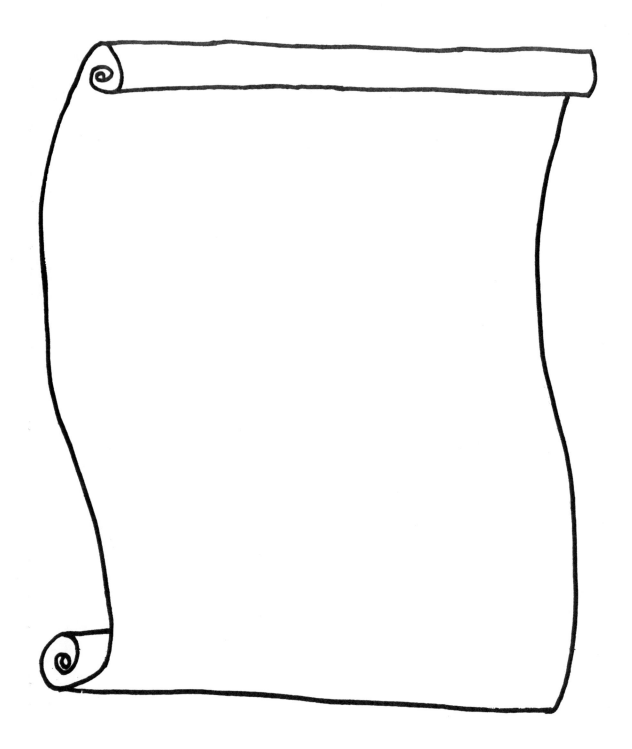

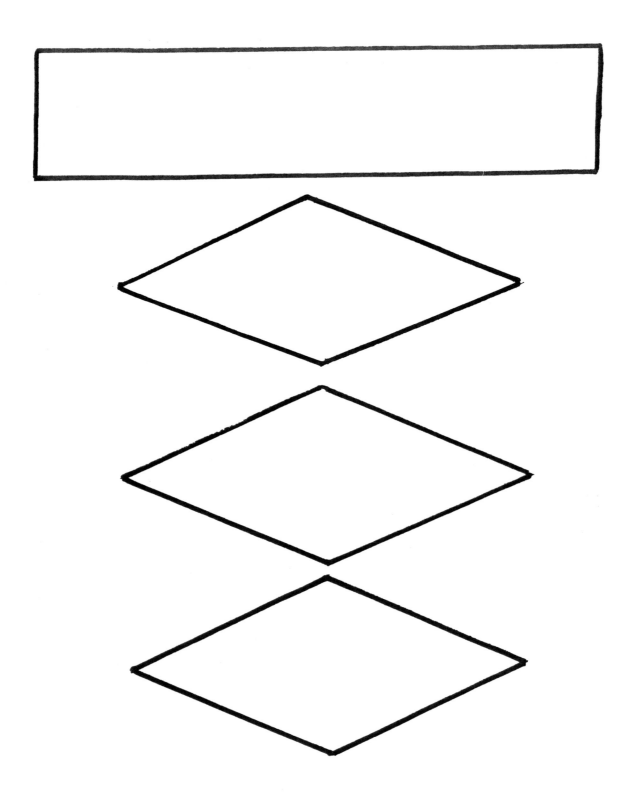

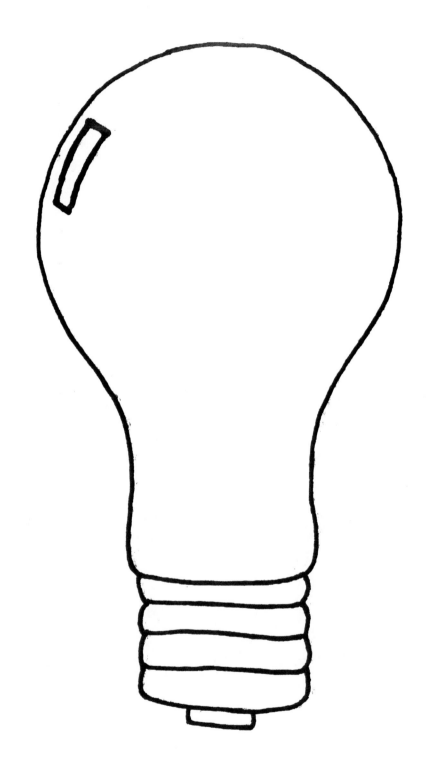

SAMPLE FLIP CHART ICONS

WHERE TO FIND
FLIP CHART ACCESSORIES
AND RESOURCES

Source	Address/Phone	Items
Acco Manufacturing	770 Acco Plaza Wheeling, IL 60090-6070 (847) 541-9500	Metal bull clips
Advantus Corporation	(800) 771-0529	Panel wall clips
Apollo Presentation Products	Ronkonkoma, NY 11779 (516) 467-8033	Easels; audiovisual equipment
Art-Phyl Creations	16250 NW 48th Avenue Miami, FL 33014-6415 (800) 327-8318	Merchandise display products
Avery-Dennison (formerly Static Images)	1 Better Way Chicopee, MA 01022 (800) 336-4766	Write-on vinyl static cling sheets
Barr Display	6170 Edgewater Drive Orlando, FL 32810 (407) 298-2277	Merchandise display supplies
Creative Presentation Resources, Inc.	P.O. Box 180487 Casselberry, FL 32718-0487 (800) 308-0399	Rubber chicken pointers; training books; trainer's tool boxes; chalkboard line tools; cartooning instructional

	(407) 695-5535 E-mail: cprbluca@ magicnet.net	videos and kits; toys, games and incentives; creative presentation techniques workshops
Crisp Publications, Inc.	1200 Hamilton Court Menlo Park, CA 94025 (800) 442-7477	Books on effective presentations
C Thru Graphics	6 Britton Drive, Box 356 Bloomfield, CT 06002 (860) 243-0303 (800) 243-8419	Pantographs; graphic supplies and tools
Da-Lite Screen, Co., Inc.	P.O. Box 137 Warsaw, IN 46581-0137 (800) 622-3737 E-mail: info@da-lite.com	Flip chart easels and audiovisual aids; easel and pad carrying cases
Dover Publications, Inc.	31 East 2nd Street Mineola, NY 11501	Clip art books
Echo Brand Products	Dallas, TX (800) 222-6462	Flip chart storage units
Fidelity Direct	5601 International Parkway P.O. Box 155 Minneapolis, MN 55440-0155 (800) 328-3034	Flat and hanging storage units; wire and cardboard roll files; tracer projectors; cardboard shipping tubes; plastic storage tubes; spray markover
Gershel Bros.	720 North 5th Street Philadelphia, PA 19123 (800) 962-5307	New and used store fixtures; display units
Hands-On Graphics	20 Sunnyside, Suite A140 Mill Valley, CA 94941 (415) 331-7393	Graphic facilitation skills workshops
Human Performance Management	5379 Broadway Oakland, CA 94618 (510) 547-1896	*Get Graphic: How to Make Visuals that Work* workshop
Keeper Corporation	6 Industrial Park Drive North Windham, CT 06256 (800) 456-4151	Elastic stretch (bungee) cords
Lee Rowan Company	1901 Lee Avenue Jackson, MO 63755 (800) 325-6150 ext 359	Modular shelving; brackets and dual-track wall mounts; flipchart caddy for markers

Lehigh Group	Allentown, PA 18106 http://www.lehighgroup	Elastic stretch (bungee) cords
MegaPrint	P.O. Box 87 Plymouth, NH 03264 (603) 536-3001	Commercially created pages from PC-generated images
Millers' School Supplies	151 Baywood Ave., Suite 101 Longwood, FL 32750-3449 (407) 767-0095	Markers; educational supplies; chalkboard compasses/line tools; incentives
National Audio-Visual Supply	One Madison Street East Rutherford, NJ 07073 (800) 222-0109 http://www.webcom/~natav/	Easels; presentation equipment/supplies
National Business Furniture	1819 Peachtree Road Atlanta, GA 30309 (800) 558-1010	Flat flipchart file storage cabinets
Office Images Trainer's Warehouse	239 Bacon Street Natick, MA 01760-9906 (508) 653-3770 (800) 299-3770	Easel pads; plastic carrying cases; portable easels; markers; rolling rulers; flip chart flat storage bins, mobile and wall hanging units; roll-on glue
Quartet	5700 Old Orchard Road Skokie, IL 60077 (847) 965-0600 http://www.quartetmfg.com	ChartScan poster scanner; flip chart easels
Staples, Inc.	8 Technology Drive P.O. Box 1020 Westboro, MA 01581 (800) 333-3330	Presentation/office supplies; easels; markers; pads
System Works	7625 Appling Center Drive Memphis, TN 38134	Dual-track wall mounts and brackets
The Reliable Corporation	P.O. Box 1502 Ottawa, IL 61350-9914 (800) 735-4000	Markers; presentation supplies
Think BIG!	960 Brook Road Conshohocken, PA 19428 (800) 487-4244	Giant-size props (clipboard)

The Trainer's Warehouse	89 Washington Avenue Natick, MA 01760 (800) 299-3770	Easels; storage units; shipping tubes; flip chart compass; large easel pad tubes; pointers; accessories
Turnkey	500 Fillmore Avenue Tonawanda, NY 14150 (800) 348-4905	Blueprint and graphic storage units
USI	33 Business Park Drive Suite 5 Branford, CT 06405-2944 (800) 243-4565	Lamination machines/supplies
Viking Office Products	13809 South Figueroa Street P.O. Box 61144 Los Angeles, CA 90061-0144 (800) 421-1222 http://www.vikingop.com	Markers; easels; presentation supplies; flat and hanging flip chart storage units
3M Commercial Office Supply Division	3M Center, Bldg. 223-3S-03 St Paul, MN 55144-1000	Flip chart pads; Post-it flip chart stickers and Easy Roll pads; Static Images plastic flip chart pads; poster size laminating systems

BIBLIOGRAPHY

BOOKS/PUBLICATIONS

Backer, L., and M. Decker. *The Presenter's EZ Graphics Kit: A Guide for the Artistically Challenged.* Mosby-Year Book, Inc., St Louis, MO, 1996.

Blitz, B. *How to Draw Blitz Cartoons.* Running Press, Philadelphia, PA, 1991.

Brandt, R. C. *Flip Charts: How to Draw Them and How to Use Them.* University Associates, Inc., San Diego, CA, 1986.

Burn, B. E. *Flip Chart Power: Secrets of the Masters.* Pfeiffer & Co., San Diego, CA, 1996.

Edwards, B. *Drawing on the Right Side of Your Brain.* J. P. Thatcher, Los Angeles, CA, 1989.

Eitington, J. E. *The Winning Trainer*, 3d ed., Gulf Publishing Co., Houston, TX, 1996.

Gautier, D. *The Creative Cartoonist: A Step-by-Step Guide for the Aspiring Amateur.* The Putnam Publishing Group, New York, NY, 1989.

Hamm, J. *Cartooning the Head and Figure.* The Putnam Publishing Group, New York, NY, 1969.

Holmes, N. *Designer's Guide to Creating Charts and Diagrams.* Watson-Guptill Publications, New York, NY, 1990.

Howard, P. J. *The Owner's Manual for the Brain: Everyday Applications from Mind-Brain Research.* Leornian Press, Austin, TX, 1994.

Kearny, L. *Graphics for Presenters: Getting Your Ideas Across.* Crisp Publications, Menlo Park, CA, 1996.

Leech, T. *How to Prepare, Stage, and Deliver Winning Presentations.* AMACOM, New York, NY, 1993.

Maddocks, P. *Cartooning for Beginners: A Step-by-Step Guide for Drawing Cartoons*. Michael O'Mara Books, Ltd., 1992.

—. *How to Draw Cartoons*. Guild Publishing, London, England, 1991.

Maulof, D. *How to Create and Deliver a Dynamic Presentation*. ASTD, Alexandria, VA, 1992.

Newstrom, J. W., and E. E. Scannell. *Games Trainers Play*. McGraw-Hill, New York, NY, 1980.

Raines, C. *Visual Aids in Business: A Guide for Effective Presentations*. Crisp Publications, Inc., Menlo Park, CA, 1989.

Robertson, B. *How to Draw Charts and Diagrams*. North Light Books, Cincinnati, OH, 1988.

Scannell, E. E. and J. W. Newstrom. *More Games Trainers Play*. McGraw-Hill, New York, NY, 1983.

—. *Still More Games Trainers Play*. McGraw-Hill, New York, NY, 1991.

—. *Even More Games Trainers Play*. McGraw-Hill, New York, NY, 1994.

Solo, D. X. *Classic Roman Alphabets: 100 Complete Fonts*. Dover Publications, New York, NY, 1983.

—. *3-D and Shaded Alphabets: 100 Complete Fonts*. Dover Publications, New York, NY, 1982.

Sonneman, M. R. *Beyond Words: A Guide to Drawing Out Ideas*. Ten Speed Press, Berkeley, CA, 1997.

Tollison, H. *Cartooning*. Walter Foster Publishing, Tustin, CA, 1989.

Westcott, J., and J. H. Landau. *A Picture's Worth 1,000 Words: A Workbook for Visual Communications*. Jossey-Bass, San Francisco, CA, 1997.

Wotzkow, H. *The Art of Hand Lettering: Its Mastery and Practice*. Dover Publications, New York, NY, 1967.

CLIP ART PUBLICATIONS

Belanger, G. C. *Ready to Use Small Frames and Borders*. Dover Publications, Mineola, NY, 1982.

—. *Ready to Use Borders on Layout Grids*. Dover Publications, Mineola, NY, 1985.

Censoni, B. *Ready to Use Humorous Spot Illustrations*. Dover Publications, Mineola, NY, 1984.

—. *Ready to Use Humorous Office Spot Illustrations*. Dover Publications, Mineola, NY, 1987.

People at Work. F&W Publications, Cincinnati, OH, 1994.

Tierney, T. *Ready to Use Travel and Tourist Illustrations*. Dover Publications, Mineola, NY, 1987.

COMPUTER CLIP ART/GRAPHICS PACKAGES

Freelance Graphics. Lotus Development Corp., Lotus North Office, 400 River Park Drive, North Reading, MA 01864 (800) 343-5414.

Masterclips: 150,000 Premium Image Collection. IMSI, San Rafael, CA (415) 257-3000.

VIDEOS

Doodle Tricks by Bruce Blitz. (See the Creative Presentation Resources, Inc. entry in Appendix C.)

Cartoon Video Kit by Bruce Blitz, (See the Creative Presentation Resources, Inc. entry in Appendix C.)

Clip Quest by HR Images, (See the Creative Presentation Resources, Inc. entry in Appendix C.)

INDEX

ABOUT THE AUTHOR

Bob Lucas is the President of Creative Presentation Resources and has been a professional trainer for 27 years. He is the author of six books.